Adventures of Honey: A Practical Teaching Guide for Elementary Teachers

Twelve complete lessons for Elementary teachers based on the award-winning *Honey* children's book series!!

DAWN LOZANO

Weeping Willow
PUBLISHING
*Honoring memories of the past
while building dreams of the future!!*

Adventures of Honey:

A Practical Teaching Guide

for Elementary Teachers

By

Dawn Lozano

Copyright © Tom C. Greer, 2010, 2018

Printed in the United States of America

All rights reserved. Permission is granted for purchaser to reproduce activity pages within this guide for their own personal use, but otherwise, no part of it may be reproduced, stored in a retrieval system or transmitted in any form or by any means, electronic, mechanical, photocopying, or recording, without the written permission of the publisher.

Published in the United States of America.   www.tomcgreer.com

THIS GUIDE IS DEDICATED TO ALL OF THE TEACHERS
WHO WORK SO HARD TO MAKE A REAL DIFFERENCE IN THE
LIVES OF THEIR STUDENTS

CONTENTS

Foreword by Tom C. Greer   vii

A New Home for Honey

Lesson 1 – Math and History   1

Lesson 2 – English/Language Arts   16

Lesson 3 – Social Studies   31

Lesson 4 – Science   39

Honey's Peanut Butter Adventure

Lesson 5 – Math   50

Lesson 6 – English/Language Arts and Social Studies   54

Lesson 7 – Geography and English/Language Arts   64

Lesson 8 – Math and Science   72

Honey Visits Grandpa Smith

Lesson 9 – Math   87

Lesson 10 – English/Language Arts and Math   95

Lesson 11 – Math   109

Lesson 12 – Science and English/Language Arts   122

About the Author   129

FOREWARD

By Tom C. Greer

Author of *A New Home for Honey, Honey's Peanut Butter Adventure,* and *Honey Visits Grandpa Smith*

Since publishing my third title in the *Adventures of Honey* series, I have wanted to have something special for teachers to use to incorporate my stories into their classroom lessons. While I have been writing lesson plans for over eighteen years, I wanted someone to write the lessons that had more training and expertise with curriculum design. I ran an ad online for a curriculum writer and Dawn Lozano responded. After conversations back and forth for a short time, I was confident that she could do the job. She has a Master of Science in Curriculum and Instruction and has been an educator for over ten years.

The lessons in this guide include everything teachers will need to successfully present them to their students. Each lesson plan includes content area/s, grade level (this could easily be altered by teachers), learning standards, concepts, time frame, materials and resources, objectives, presentation/introduction, interest building, content development, summary/closure, evaluation and extension activities.

There are four lessons from each of my three current titles in the *Adventures of Honey* series and all content subject areas are represented including Math, Science, English/Language Arts, and Social Studies.

My hope is that you will use these lessons to stimulate a love of learning in your elementary students. Stories like mine offer so much more than just a heart-warming memory of a pet, they can teach lifelong lessons in a fun way that students enjoy.

Lesson 1: A New Home for Honey – Math and History

Content Area: History/Mathematics

Grade Level: 2nd – 3rd

Learning Standards: Interpret time lines

                        Tell and write time shown on analog and digital clocks

Concepts: time and chronology

Time Frame: 50 minutes

MATERIALS AND RESOURCES:

1. *A New Home for Honey* by Tom Greer
2. Analog clock
3. Digital clock
4. Pre-written analog clocks with times 1:00 to 9:00
5. Pre-written digital clocks with times 1:00 to 9:00
6. Large chart paper
7. Writing utensils
8. Attached worksheets

OBJECTIVES:

The students will be able to…
1. Interpret and sequence a time line
2. Read time
3. Tell time
4. Write time in both analog and digital forms

PRESENTATION/INTRODUCTION: attention getter

Show the students a clock and ask them "What is this? What do we use it for? Why is it important to tell time? How do you tell time? Why would we need to know what time it is?" Hold a discussion about the importance of knowing how to read and write time. Mention how we have to be at school or work at a certain time, how we make appointments for certain times and some people take medication at certain times. If we didn't know how to read time or didn't know what time it was we might not get where we need to be or get what we need on time.

Show the cover of the book and read the title, author and illustrator. Show the back of the book, spine of the book and its title page. Compare the cover and title page: are they the same or different? Again, read the title of the book, the author and the illustrator to the students.

Teacher reads "A New Home for Honey" by Tom C. Greer. During the read aloud, the teacher points out the order of events that are occurring, for example: "Honey had a home where her mother lived first but is now in a new home with Tommy. Let's see what happens to Honey next." As the teacher reads the story, he/she should point out how most of the pictures are happening during the daytime but the story ends at night. We can tell it is night time because Tommy and Honey are going to sleep.

Upon completion of the read aloud, the teacher will use the large chart paper to answer these questions:

Title the chart paper: Honey's Timeline

3 columns: picture, answers, time

1. What happened to Honey first?
2. Where did she go next?
3. After she was at her new home what happened?
4. After she ate, what happened next?
5. What did Tommy give her to sleep in?
6. Where did she wind up sleeping at the end of the story?

As the teacher writes down the events that occurred to Honey, be sure to write in short answers and/or draw pictures. Here's an example of what the teacher's chart paper may look like:

1.    Honey lived with her mom until Tommy came to pick her up.

2.    She then went to her new home with Tommy and his mommy.

3.    Tommy's mom fed Honey and gave her water.

4.  or    Tommy and his mom named her Honey and not Apricot.

5. 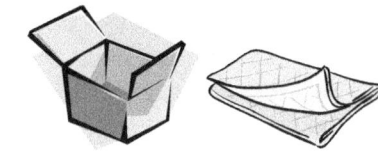 Tommy gave her a box and blanket to sleep in.

6.  Honey went to the bed to sleep with Tommy.

Use the book as a reference for the students: as the student responds and verbally answers, turn to the page in the book or allow the student to find the pages.

Tell the students we will be adding clock times to the Honey timeline in just a bit.

INTEREST BUILDING: why it is important

Ask students who knows how to tell time? Can you read an analog clock? Can you read a digital clock? Which is easier to read? Why? Who is wearing a watch today? What sort of watch is it? If there are enough watches in the classroom have the students sort them, then count how many were each type. Ask the students to brainstorm other places we find clocks and other reasons we would want to keep track of time.

Show students analog clock and define what each hand is for: large hand is for the minutes and little hand is for the hours. Mention hours take a longer time minutes and manipulate the analog clock to show the movement of the hands. Demonstrate how the large hand moves faster than the small hand. At this time, pick a volunteer to come up and manipulate the clock. Manipulate the clock to show each hour: as the clock is moved to the next hour, students should say the hour aloud "12 o'clock, 1 o'clock etc."

Now show the digital clock and define what the numbers stand for. First set of numbers is the hour and the second set of numbers is the minutes. Manipulate the digital to tell the time for each hour and have the students say the hour aloud as before.

Choose a few students to come up and manipulate the clocks and match each other's times. I.e. analog is 1 o'clock and digital has to match.

CONTENT DEVELOPMENT: modeling/guided practice

1. Put the clocks away.
2. Tell the students they will be playing a time game where they will have to match analog and digital clock times.

3. Half of the children are given an analog clock and the other half digital clocks. Each of the clocks have the times 1 o'clock to 9 o'clock already written on them.
4. The game starts off with one students saying "I have 1 o'clock, who has the same time?" The other student with the matching clock then says, "I have 1 o'clock too."
5. This process continues until everyone has had a turn.
6. Students at this time can be put into pairs by their matching times or groups or left to work the next part of the activity alone. (Teacher's preference)
7. Refer back to Honey's timeline.
8. Tell the students that Honey's timeline begins at 4:00

9. Give each child, pairs or each of the groups the attached sheet with six clocks.
10. They are to draw a picture of the events we listed on the chart paper and write the time in both analog and digital forms. Remind the students that each event happened on the hour, one hour after the other starting at 4:00.

SUMMARY/CLOSURE: review

1. Once everyone's sheet is filled out regroup.
2. Share with another person, pair or group.
3. Share with the whole group.
4. Ask what their experiences were writing down both forms. Was it easier to write down the analog form than they thought?
5. Ask why it might be important to know when things happened to Honey?
6. Why do we need to know the time for ourselves?

EVALUATION: assess

1. Students can be asked what happened at 4:00, 6:00, etc.
2. Students can match analog and digital times.
3. Students can write down certain times dictated by teacher or written as "5 o'clock" and put in analog or digital form.

EXTENSION: center and homework

- Picture cards to sequence "A New Home for Honey"
- Matching analog and digital clock times
- Manipulate analog clock to match digital times
- Leave blank analog and digital clock sheets in a center to be filled out

- Homework: Teacher-made sheet with both blank analog and digital clocks to fill out next to each question.

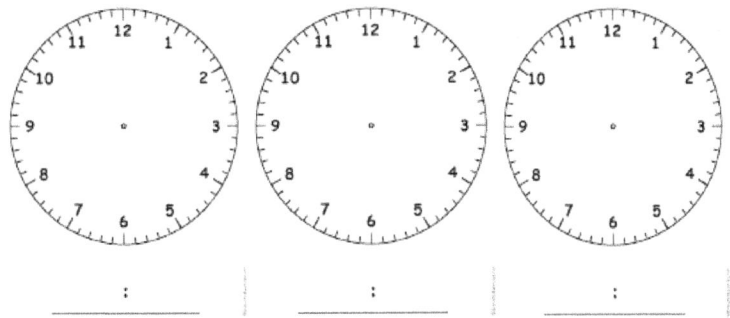

Questions:
1. What time do you get up for school?
2. What time do you get up on the weekend?
3. What time do you go to sleep?

OR

Timeline your day from morning till evening by the hour & write these times.

"A New Home for Honey" 2nd to 3rd grade Chronology & Time lesson
Start with 4 o'clock (write analog and digital times).
Then, sequence Honey's day with pictures and times.

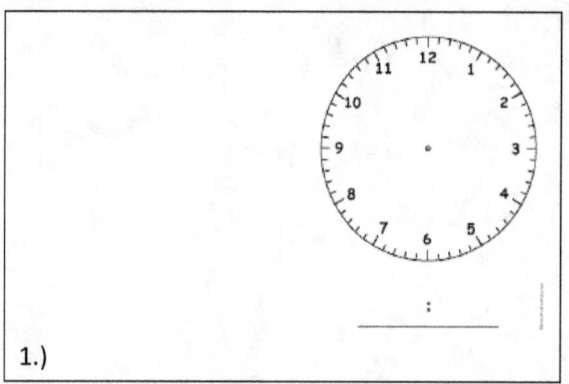

1.)

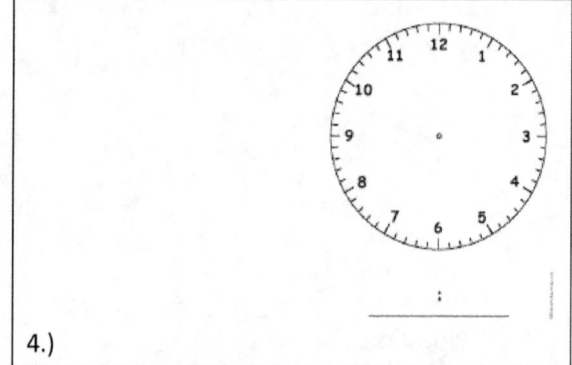

4.)

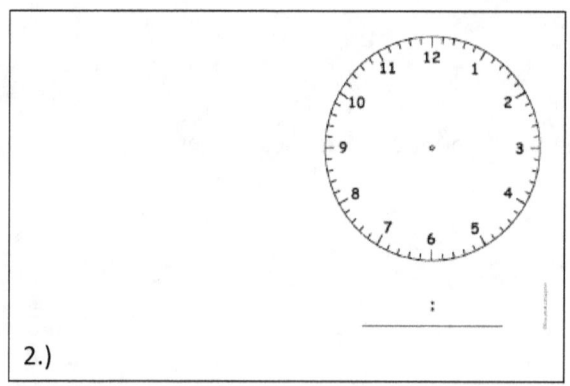

2.)

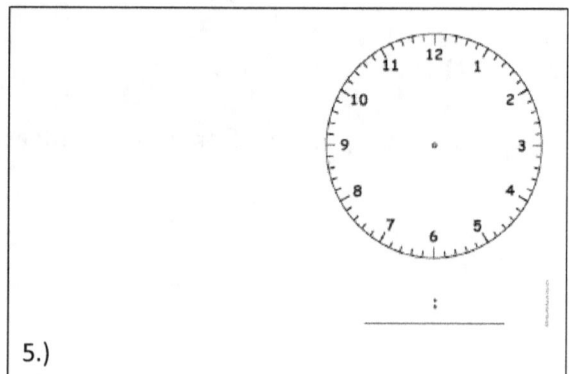

5.)

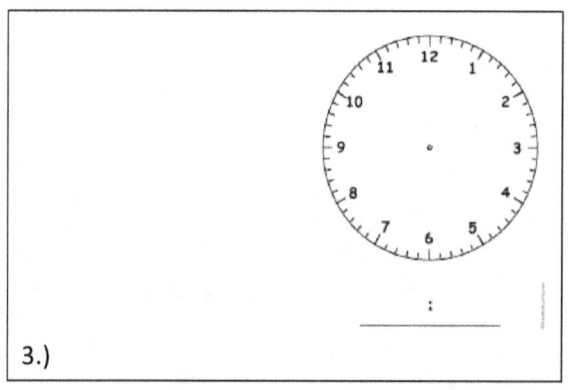

3.)

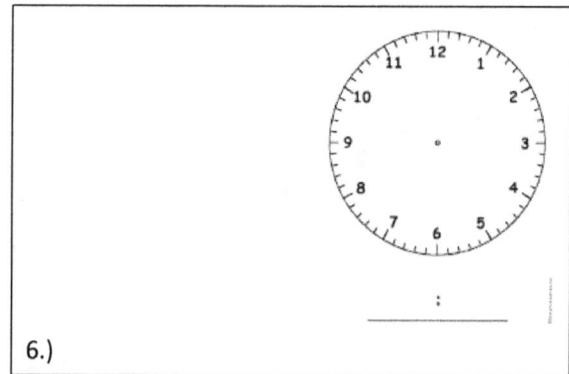

6.)

"A New Home for Honey" matching game worksheet
Teacher: write times 1 o'clock to 9 o'clock on each type of clock, cut & laminate

Use these clocks for the matching game.

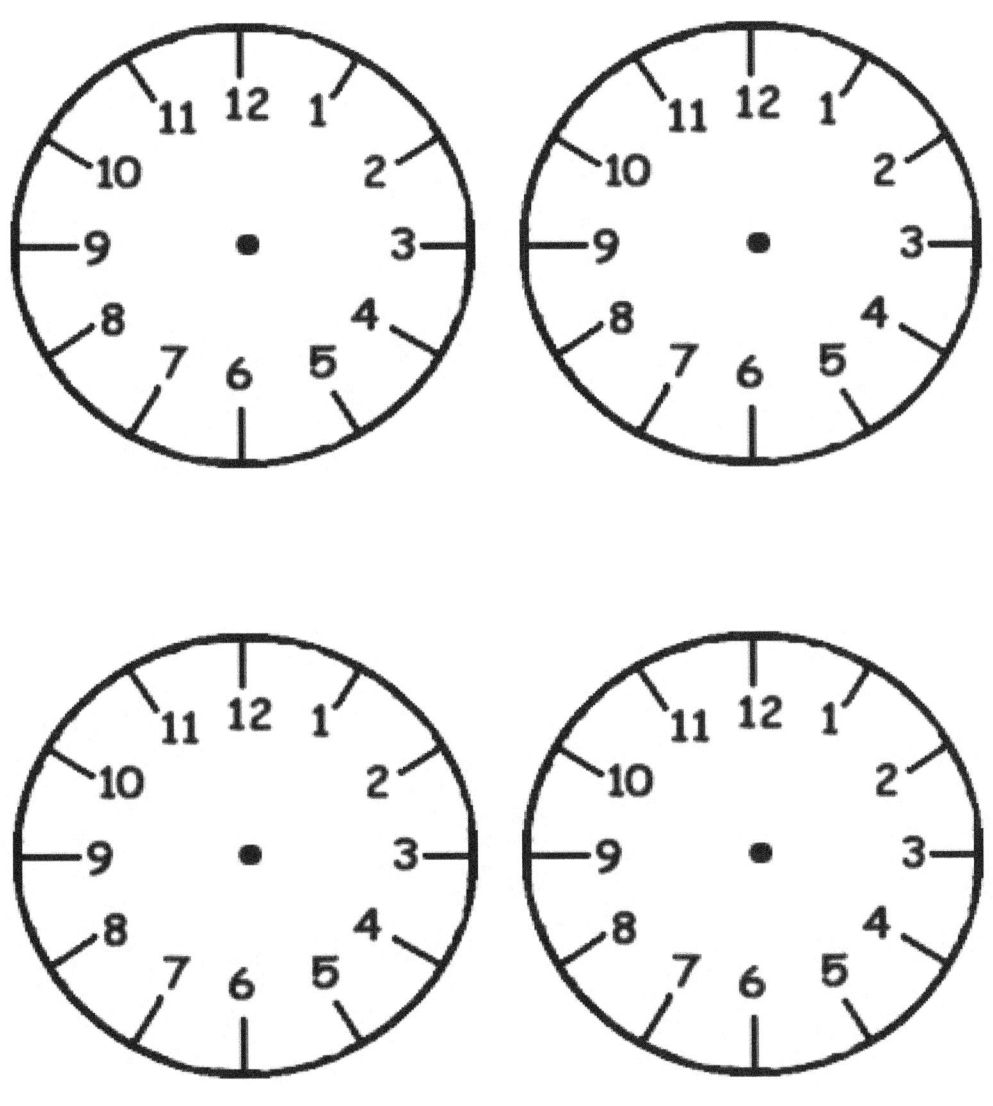

"A New Home for Honey" matching game worksheet
Teacher: write times 1 o'clock to 9 o'clock on each type of clock, cut & laminate

8

"A New Home for Honey" Sequencing cards for center.
Cut out pictures, words and times.
Match pictures to words to digital times.
Then, write time in analog form: these cards may be laminated for continued use or make several copies.

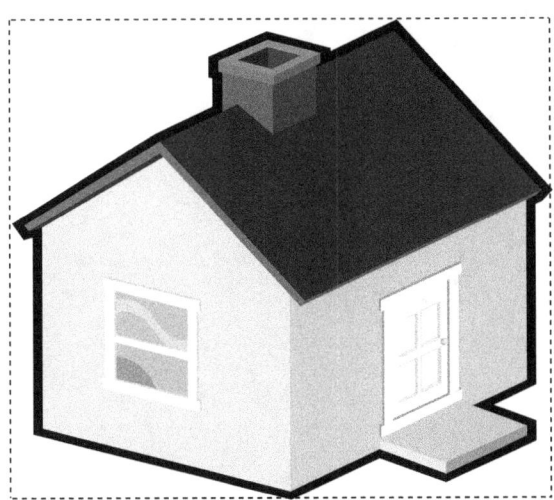

"A New Home for Honey" Sequencing cards for center.
Cut out pictures, words and times.
Match pictures to words to digital times.
Then, write time in analog form: these cards may be laminated for continued use or make several copies.

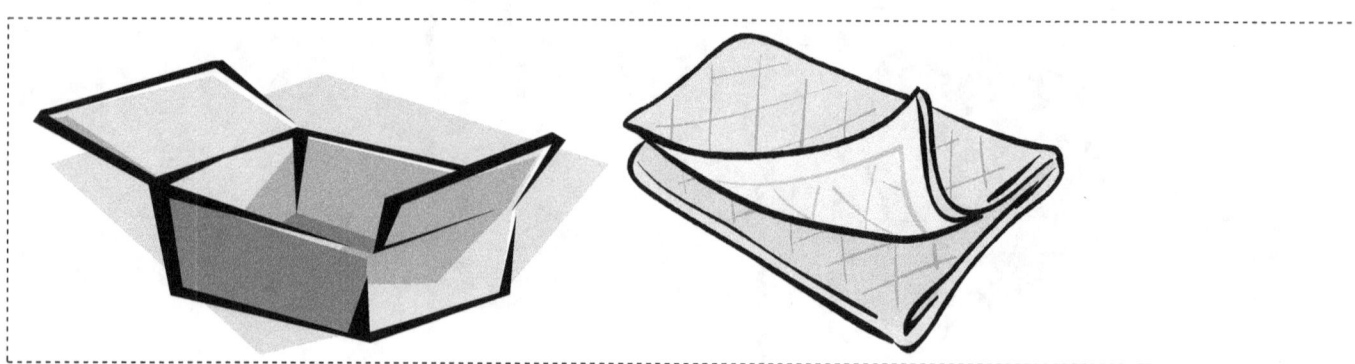

"A New Home for Honey" Sequencing cards for center.
Cut out pictures, words and times.
Match pictures to words to digital times.
Then, write time in analog form: these cards may be laminated for continued use or make several copies.

Honey lived with her mom until Tommy came to pick her up.

She then went to her new home with Tommy and his mommy.

"A New Home for Honey" Sequencing cards for center.
Cut out pictures, words and times.
Match pictures to words to digital times.
Then, write time in analog form: these cards may be laminated for continued use or make several copies.

Tommy's mom fed Honey and gave her water.

Tommy and his mom named her Honey and not Apricot.

Tommy gave her a box and blanket to sleep in.

"A New Home for Honey" Sequencing cards for center.
Cut out pictures, words and times.
Match pictures to words to digital times.
Then, write time in analog form: these cards may be laminated for continued use or make several copies.

Honey went to the bed to sleep with Tommy.

4:00

5:00

6:00

"A New Home for Honey" Sequencing cards for center.
Cut out pictures, words and times.
Match pictures to words to digital times.
Then, write time in analog form: these cards may be laminated for continued use or make several copies.

7:00

8:00

9:00

"A New Home for Honey" Sequencing cards for center.
Cut out pictures, words and times.
Match pictures to words to digital times.
Then, write time in analog form: these cards may be laminated for continued use or make several copies.

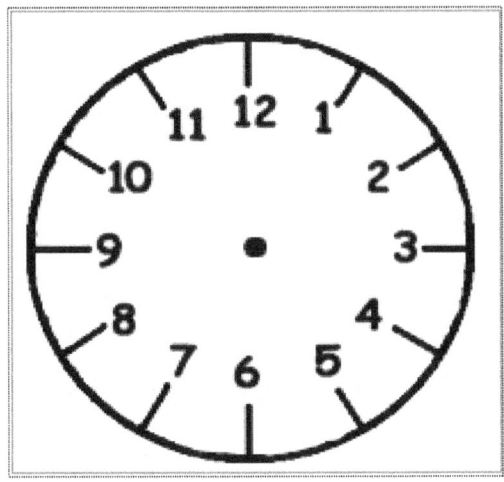
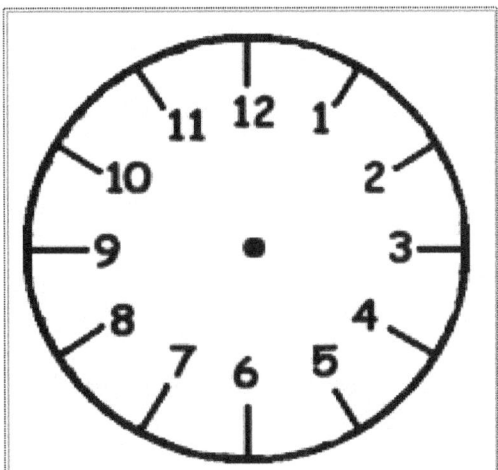
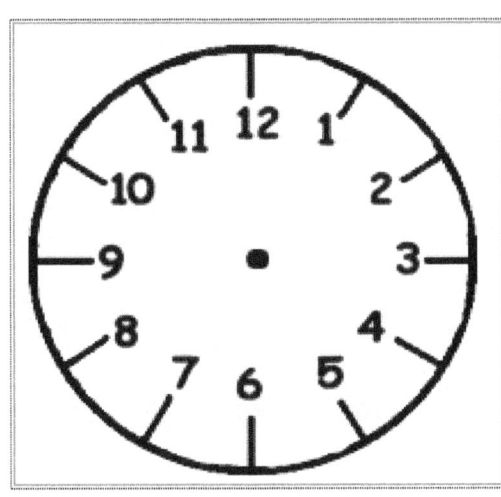
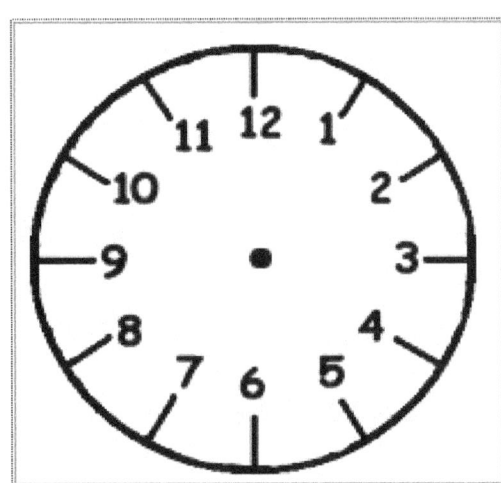
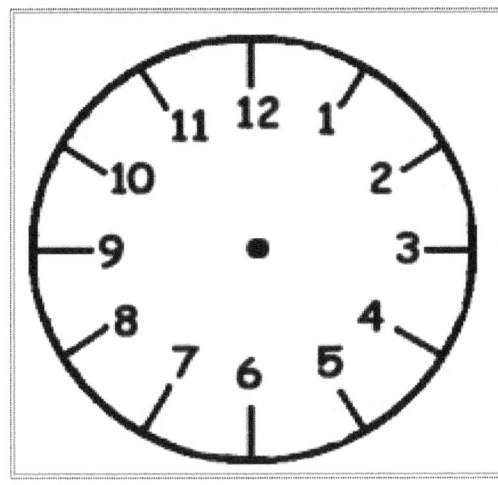
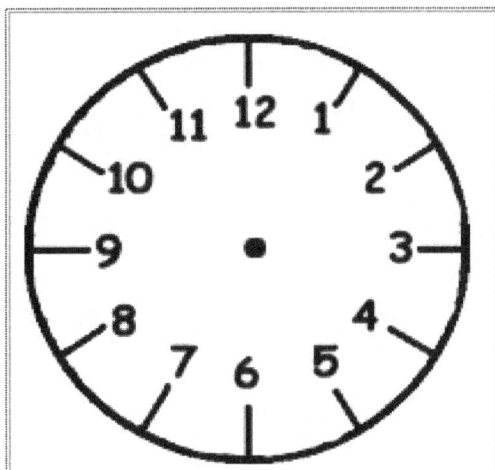

Lesson 2: A New Home for Honey – English Language Arts

Content Area: Language Arts/Vocabulary

Grade Level: Kindergarten – 1st

Learning Standards: Identify opposites

Concepts: what is an opposite, identify and name a variety of opposites, improve vocabulary

Time Frame: 40 minutes

MATERIALS AND RESOURCES:

1. *A New Home for Honey* by Tom Greer
2. Large chart paper
3. Writing utensils, markers, crayons
4. Attached sheets: opposites drawing sheets(one per pair/group), matching game (one per pair//group), fill in the blank (one per student)
5. For center, use attached sheets as well: matching by drawing line and manipulate dog to do opposite moves
6. scissors

OBJECTIVES:

The students will be able to…
1. identify opposites
2. act out/demonstrate an opposite
3. distinguish between opposites
4. match opposites
5. use opposites vocabulary

PRESENTATION/INTRODUCTION: attention getter

Ask the students if they know what an opposite is. Teacher then defines opposite as something being totally different. At this time the teacher could point out some opposites in the classroom such as some-one standing and some-one sitting or the lights being off and then on. Have the students name the opposites as they are being presented. Now give the students a few words for the students to guess the opposites for. Here are some examples, hot and _____, big and _____, fast and _____, etc. Now show the cover of the book to the students and tell them we will be looking for opposites during the story.

Show the cover of the book and read the title, author and illustrator. Show the back of the book, spine of the book and its title page. Compare the cover and title page: are they the same or different? Again, read the title of the book, the author and the illustrator to the students.

Teacher reads "A New Home for Honey" by Tom C. Greer. During the read aloud, the teacher points out Honey in Tommy's arms up high then on the ground down low, Honey walking and running, Honey in the box and out of the box, etc.

Upon completion of the read aloud, the teacher will use the large chart paper and title it "Opposites". Go through the pages of the book and have the students tell you all the opposites they see from Honey, Tommy and his mom.

Your list may look like this:

Honey jumping/still

Honey up high/down low

Tommy happy/worried

Tommy and mom standing/sitting

Honey out of the box/in the box

Honey and Tommy awake/asleep

Now that this list is complete, have the students act out the opposites. The students should also say what they are doing and name the opposite they are to do next. Once the list has been acted out the students may sit back down.

INTEREST BUILDING: **why it is important**

Tell the students we will now act out our own opposites. The teacher will give the word and students are to guess and act out the opposite.

Here is a list of words the teacher can use with example student may do:

Up/down

Wiggle/still

Arms up/down

Run/walk

Hands open/closed

Eyes open/shut

Leg up/down

Hands close together/far apart

Shoulders up/down

Have the students sit down and discuss their experiences with guessing the opposites for the teacher's words. Did they find it easy or difficult to guess what to do? How did they know what the opposite was? Was the second move they did the total opposite from the first move?

Write down the moves the students made if not done already and review the list.

CONTENT DEVELOPMENT: modeling/guided practice

1. Ask students to now get into pair or groups and pass out the matching the opposite cards and the blank boxes sheet to draw the opposites in. The pairs/groups will also need writing and drawing utensils.
2. The students will work together and play the game first. They are to cut out the cards and find the matching pairs of opposites. The cards could be split into right and left sections and two students could ask one another for the opposite card. Or the cards could be placed face down and turned over until all the opposites are found.
3. Once the game has been place the students may take turns drawing the opposites named in their blank opposite sheet provided.

SUMMARY/CLOSURE: review

1. Once everyone has played the game and drawn their opposites, share there answer sheets aloud and check.
2. Ask questions about the opposites: Were there any opposites that where hard to guess? Were there any opposites that were hard to draw?
3. Could you come up with a pair of opposites yourself?
4. Could you show us a pair of opposites by acting them out?

EVALUATION: assess

1. Students will fill in the blank with an opposite word, a picture my be drawn on the side (1-10)
2. Review the sheet with the student.
3. Give the student a variety of words and have him/her act out the opposite such as eyes open/closed, point finger up/down, etc.

EXTENSION: center and homework

- Match opposites game: attached sheets
- Find opposites in a magazine and cut them out
- Place mirrors in a center and have students make opposite facial expressions such as happy/sad, glad/mad, etc.

- Lay out blank opposite page for drawing in a center or allow the students to cut magazine pictures and place in boxes of sheet instead.
- Use provided sheets (2) and erasable markers in a center to match opposites by drawing a line from left to right.

- Homework:

1. Turn your lights off and on

2. Open and close a door

3. Touch something cold and something warm (ask adult for help)

4. Run then walk

5. Sit then stand

6. Get under and in the blanket and then come out

7. Put your shoe on then take it off

8. Now, draw a picture of you doing one of the sets of opposites and write a sentence telling us what you are doing.

"New Home for Honey" 1st grade
Laminate and put in a center with erasable marker & match the opposites
Larger cards are to place paper dog on/off, on top/bottom, inside/outside

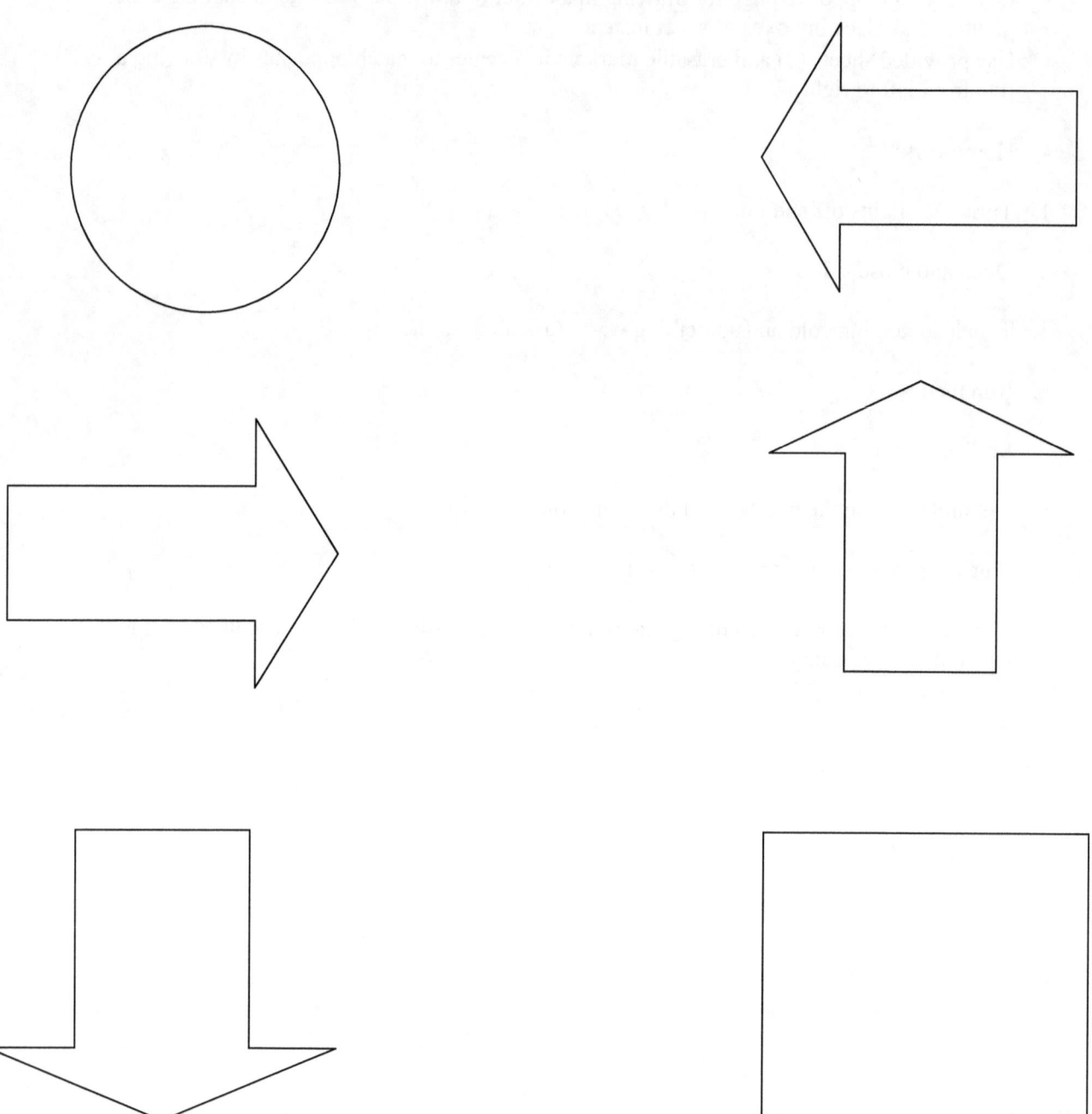

"New Home for Honey" 1st grade
Laminate and put in a center with erasable marker & match the opposites
Larger cards are to place paper dog on/off, on top/bottom, inside/outside

21

"New Home for Honey" 1st grade
Laminate and put in a center with erasable marker & match the opposites
Larger cards are to place paper dog on/off, on top/bottom, inside/outside

"New Home for Honey" 1st grade
Laminate and put in a center with erasable marker & match the opposites
Larger cards are to place paper dog on/off, on top/bottom, inside/outside

"New Home for Honey" 1st grade
Laminate and put in a center with erasable marker & match the opposites
Larger cards are to place paper dog on/off, on top/bottom, inside/outside

"New Home for Honey" 1st grade
Laminate and put in a center with erasable marker & match the opposites
Larger cards are to place paper dog on/off, on top/bottom, inside/outside

"A New Home for Honey" 1st grade
Fill in the blank with the opposite

Fill in the blank with the opposite word.

1.  boys
_____

2. ⬆ up
_____

3. 🔸 little
_____

4. 📦 full
_____

5. 🐌 slow
_____

6.  right
_____

7. 🚪 open
_____

8. 🏃 running
_____

9. 🧍 man
_____

10.  squiggly
_____

"A New Home for Honey" 1st grade
Draw opposite sheets
Matching game cards
Fill in the blank with the opposite

happy	sad
awake	asleep
sit	stand
run	walk

"A New Home for Honey" 1st grade
Draw opposite sheets
Matching game cards
Fill in the blank with the opposite

black	white
striped	polka-dots
fast	slow
tall	short

"A New Home for Honey" 1st grade
Draw opposite sheets
Matching game cards
Fill in the blank with the opposite

29

"A New Home for Honey" 1st grade
Draw opposite sheets
Matching game cards
Fill in the blank with the opposite

Lesson 3: A New Home for Honey – Social Studies

Content Area: Social Studies/Economics

Grade Level: Kindergarten – 1st

Learning Standards: Identify basic human and pet needs

Make choices between wants and needs

Concepts: what are needs to sustain life, what are wants, what do humans and pets need, compare and contrast

Time Frame: 40 minutes

MATERIALS AND RESOURCES:

1. *A New Home for Honey* by Tom Greer
2. Large chart paper: Venn diagram pre-drawn, one sheet for listing Honey's Needs, one sheet for human needs
3. Writing utensils
4. Attached worksheets: Venn diagram (one per student), sorting cards (one per pair/group), draw line from human/pet to needs sheet (one per student)
5. Scissors (per pair/per group)

OBJECTIVES:

The students will be able to…
1. identify basic human needs
2. identify basic pet needs
3. distinguish between wants and needs

PRESENTATION/INTRODUCTION: attention getter

Ask the students if they have been at the store with their parents and asked for something they wanted but mom/dad said "no." Discuss what sort of things they were asking for. Ask the students if they know why their parents said "no." Explain to the students that we can not always get everything we want because our parents have to make sure we get everything we need first. Our parents have to make sure we have a place to live, food to eat and have clothes to wear every day. Explain to the students that if they ever get a pet those needs have to be met too. Show the book cover and point to Honey. Tell the students that this is Honey and she is going to live with a new family that will meet all her needs so that she can be happy and healthy just like her owner.

Show the cover of the book and read the title, author and illustrator. Show the back of the book, spine of the book and its title page. Compare the cover and title page: are they the same or different? Again, read the title of the book, the author and the illustrator to the students.

Teacher reads "A New Home for Honey" by Tom C. Greer. During the read aloud, the teacher may stress that everyone needs a home during the part when Honey moves from one house to the other. Ask the students, "Who is going to take care of Honey's needs? Does Honey need the food that Tommy's mom is giving her? What do you think about all that running around Honey gets to do in the backyard, do you think that exercise is good?" Point out different needs that are being met throughout the story.

Upon completion of the read aloud, the teacher will use the large chart paper entitled "Honey's Needs" to make a list. Go through the pages of the book and have the students tell you all the needs Honey had.

Your list may look like this:

- Home/shelter
- Food
- Yard/exercise
- Love
- Bed

Ask the students to think of other things Honey is going to need and add them to the list.

- Water
- Collar
- Medicine
- Veterinarian
- Poop bags/ puppy pads

INTEREST BUILDING: **why it is important**

Ask students to now make a list of what humans need to live. Explain to the students that these are things we need to live every day.

Your list should consist of these things:

- Food
- Water
- Home/shelter
- Exercise
- Love
- Medicine
- Doctor

Review the list and ask the students what would happen if they did not get one of these things. Discuss how not everyone needs medicine but some of us do and how we all need to see the doctor to check on our health.

Now ask the students to come up with a list of things they want.

Your lists will probably consist of these things:

- Toys
- Games
- Movies
- Etc.

Review the list and ask the students what would happen if they did not get one of these things. Tell them how these items are just to fill up our time and entertain us. We do not need these types of things to live.

CONTENT DEVELOPMENT: modeling/guided practice

1. Ask students to now think of what Honey and a person both need. Turn to the Venn diagram on the large chart paper. Look at both the list and see what they had in common. Write those things in the center of the diagram.

- Food
- Water
- Shelter
- Exercise
- Love.
- Doctor

2. Now ask the students to list what Honey needs that a human doesn't need.
    - Dog bowl
    - Collar
    - Dog house
    - Treats
3. Now ask the students to list what a person needs that Honey doesn't.
    - Bath tub
    - Bed
    - Education
4. Once the diagram is filled out, the teacher may pair up the students or put them into small groups. At this time, they should be given a set of sorting cards to be cut out and sorted into human and pet needs.
5. Tell the students that there are two cards that humans and pets share. Those go into a separate pile. They are the doctor card and the heart/love card.
6. The students may glue these onto separate sheets of paper or simply keep them in piles.

SUMMARY/CLOSURE: review

1. Once everyone's cards are sorted re-group and check their work.

2. Ask questions like what they had in common, what did Honey need that a human didn't and vice-versa.
3. What would happen if we didn't get what we needed and only got what we wanted?
4. Why do our parents tell us no when we ask for wants?
5. Can we always get what we want? Why not?
6. Is it better to get what you need or what you want? Why?

EVALUATION: assess

1. Students will draw a line from the person/pet to their need (attached sheet).
2. Review the sheet with the student.

EXTENSION: center and homework

- Sort picture cards into wants and needs piles
- Cut out pictures from a magazine and glue under wants and needs titles
- In the dramatic play are make sure to have wants and needs items available: food, games, clothes, money, etc.

- Homework: draw a picture of a want and a need

Draw a line from the person or dog to their needs.

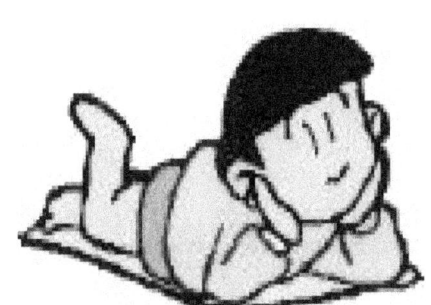

"A New Home for Honey" Kindergarten – 1st
Human and Pet Needs Sorting Picture Cards

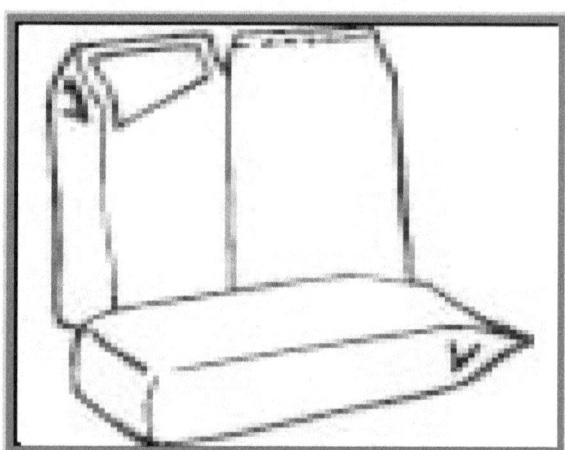

"A New Home for Honey" Kindergarten – 1st
Human and Pet Needs Sorting Picture Cards

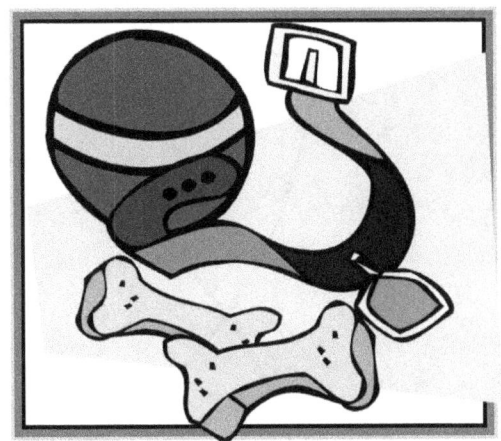

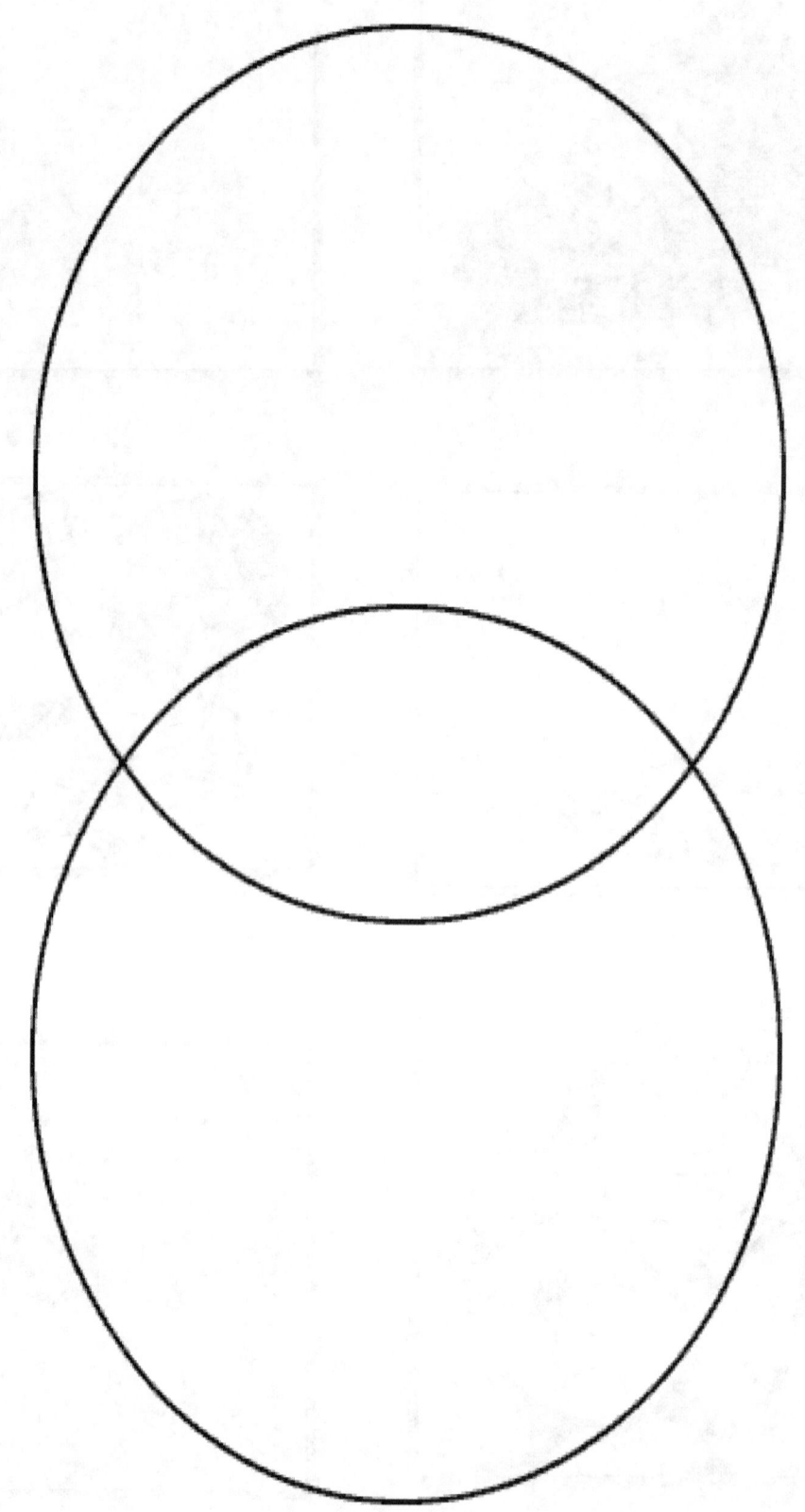

Lesson 4: A New Home for Honey – Science

Content Area: Science

Grade Level: Kindergarten – 1st

Learning Standards: Identify and name body parts of humans and animals

        Sort organisms according to their parts and characteristics

        Parts of a whole

Concepts: living organisms are systems that have parts; organisms are composed of unique body parts

Time Frame: 40 minutes

MATERIALS AND RESOURCES:

1. *A New Home for Honey* by Tom Greer
2. chart paper
3. writing utensil
4. Attached worksheets: sorting cards (one per pair/group): another set of these same cards will also need to be placed on card stock or construction paper and laminated (one per student for bingo game), vocabulary cards (one set for constructing human and dog), sorting sheet (one per pair/group)
5. Human body made out of construction paper: head with eyes, nose, mouth and hair, ears are separate, arms, hands, legs, feet, body/torso: to be used as a puzzle
6. Dog body made out of construction paper: head with eyes, separate ears, nose, mouth with whiskers, 4 legs with 4 paws attached, body/torso, tail: to be used as a puzzle
7. Bingo markers such as unifix cubes, tiles, etc.: enough for a class to play a bingo game

OBJECTIVES:

The students will be able to…
1. identify and name human body parts
2. identify and name dog body parts
3. construct and human body
4. construct a dog body
5. label body parts
6. sort body parts

PRESENTATION/INTRODUCTION: attention getter

Tell the students to look at their neighbor's face. Ask them: does your neighbor have eyes, a nose, a mouth, etc. Point out how humans are made with the same body parts. Ask the students if they have a tail, whiskers or paws? How do you think it would feel to have those sorts of body parts? What would you do with a tail? How would it feel to have paws instead of hands? Show the book cover and point to Honey. Tell the students that this is Honey and she is a dog. She has here own body parts just like we humans do. Ask the students to pay attention to the people in the book and Honey. What are they doing with their body parts?

Show the cover of the book and read the title, author and illustrator. Show the back of the book, spine of the book and its title page. Compare the cover and title page: are they the same or different? Again, read the title of the book, the author and the illustrator to the students.

Teacher reads "A New Home for Honey" by Tom C. Greer. During the read aloud, the teacher may point out "What is Honey wagging? What body part is Tommy using to carry Honey? What is Honey standing on? What is Tommy using to walk? What is Honey using to run?"

Upon completion of the read aloud, the teacher will go through the pages of the book. This time instead of reading the story the students will hold a discussion on what Honey, Tommy and Tommy's mother are doing with their body parts.

INTEREST BUILDING: why it is important

Students will now help make a list, on the large chart paper, of what humans can do with their body parts.

Your list should consist of these things:

- Eyes: to see
- Arms: to hold, to carry
- Legs: to run, walk, jump
- Nose: to breathe

Review the list and ask the students. Now ask the students to come up with any other things we can do with these body parts. Once that is complete the students will now help make a list of dog body parts and what they can do with them.

Your lists will probably consist of these things:

- Tail: wag, balance
- Legs: walk, run, jump
- Paws: digging, holding
- Nose: smelling, sniffing

Review the list and ask the students if they can think of anything else a dog may be able to do with their body parts.

CONTENT DEVELOPMENT: modeling/guided practice

1. Tell students they will now put person and a dog together using their own unique body parts.
2. Choose students to come up and construct both or a choice of the dog and/or the person. They will be using the pre-made construction paper puzzles at this time.
3. Once everyone has had a chance to construct both or one of the puzzles, have a few students come up and use the attached vocabulary cards to label each body part.
4. Repeat this process a few times.
5. Remove the labels and ask the students to compare the body parts of the human and dog.
   - Do they both have eyes? How many?
   - Do they both have a nose? Where and how many?
   - Which has a tail?
   - Which has hands? Which has paws? Are they similar? How?
6. After the comparison and contrast session, pass out a body parts bingo card to each child.
7. Make sure the teacher has his/her own set of cards to show the body part picture when called.
8. Teacher begins to call out body parts and shows picture.
9. Students mark their cards until it is full.
10. Upon completion, the students may say "Body Bingo!"
11. Remove bingo markers and pick up cards.

SUMMARY/CLOSURE: review

1. Once everyone's cards are picked up. Have the students stand up.
2. Have the students blink their eyes, open their mouth, hop on one leg, etc.
3. Have the students pretend to be dogs and dig with their paws, way their tail, hop on two hind legs, etc.
4. Have a few students tell the class what to do with their body parts such as clap your hands and stomp your feet.
5. Take out the construction paper puzzles one more time and construct them the wrong way, putting a tail on the person and switching legs and feet. Hold a little discussion on why we are not made this way and how each of us is unique.

EVALUATION: assess

1. Students will cut and sort body part under appropriate heading.
2. Students may also write the word next to the body part and if there is room they may write something that is done with that body part.
3. Review the sheet with the student.
4. Have the students share their work.

EXTENSION: center and homework

- Sort picture cards into human and dog body parts
- Cut out pictures from magazines people and animals, then label their body parts

- If possible have puzzles which deal with body parts, dressing clothes or animals
- Construct human and animals with body parts
- Leave magnifying glasses and mirrors in center for children to look at themselves closely
- Draw a picture of a friend's face and label their facial features
- Match body part to word for humans and animals: can use laminated construction paper puzzles used for lesson and vocabulary cards
- Make a laminated version of the sorting cards and sorting sheet that goes with this lesson in a center for review

- Homework: draw a picture of a family member and label their head, body, arms, legs, etc.

- Draw a picture of your pet and label his/her body parts.

"A New Home For Honey" Kinder – 1st Human and Dog Body Parts sorting sheet
Teacher can use copy of bingo card for this activity.

Human Body Parts

Dog Body Parts

"A New Home for Honey" Kinder – 1ˢᵗ Body Parts Bingo and sorting sheet

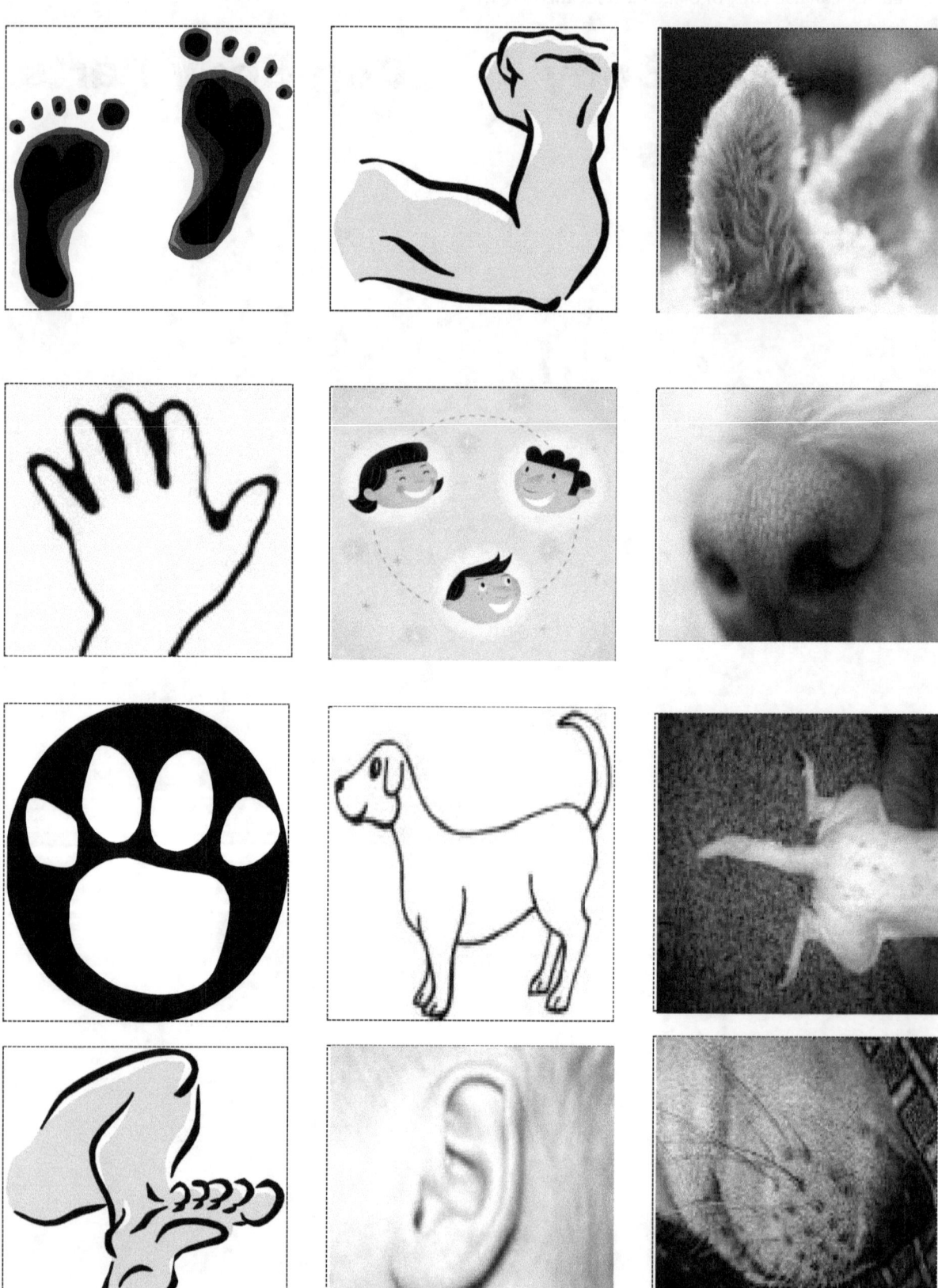

44

"A New Home for Honey" Kindergarten – 1st grade
Vocabulary Cards

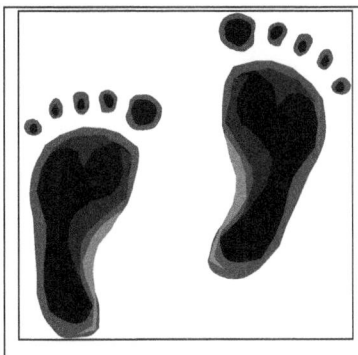 **feet with toes**

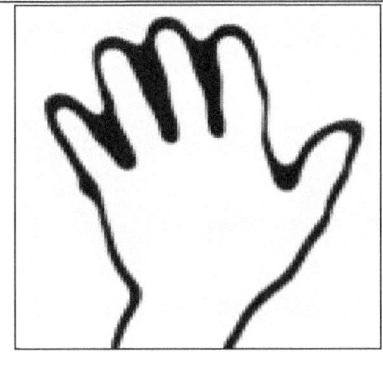 **hand with fingers**

 **paw**

"A New Home for Honey" Kindergarten – 1st grade
Vocabulary Cards

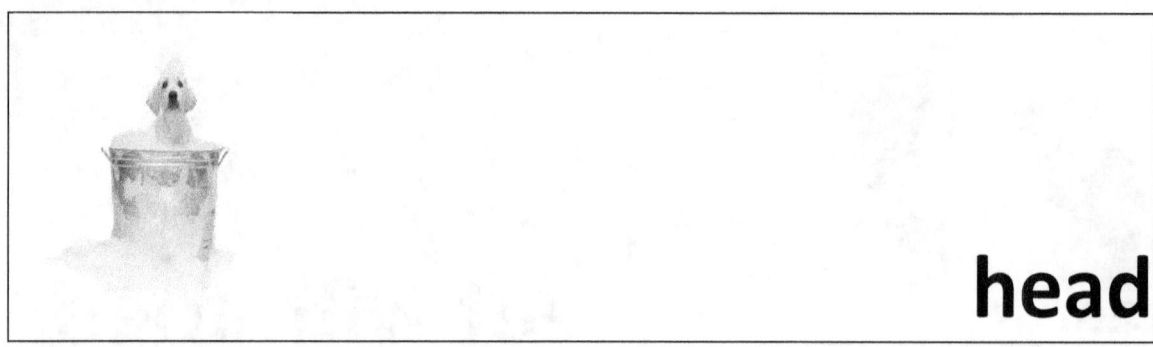 **head**

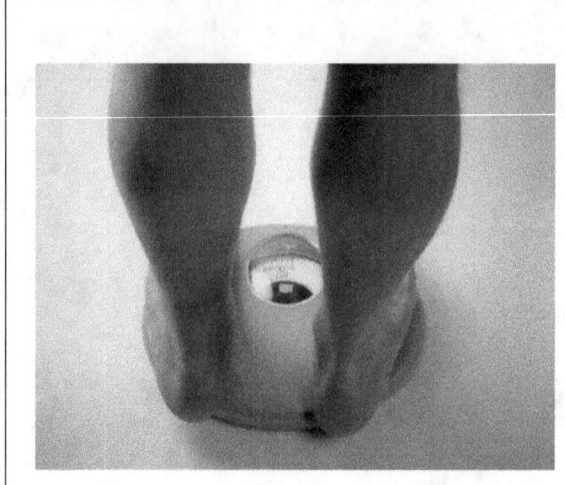 **leg**

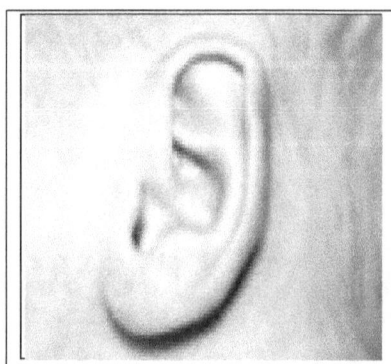 **ear**

"A New Home for Honey" Kindergarten – 1st grade
Vocabulary Cards

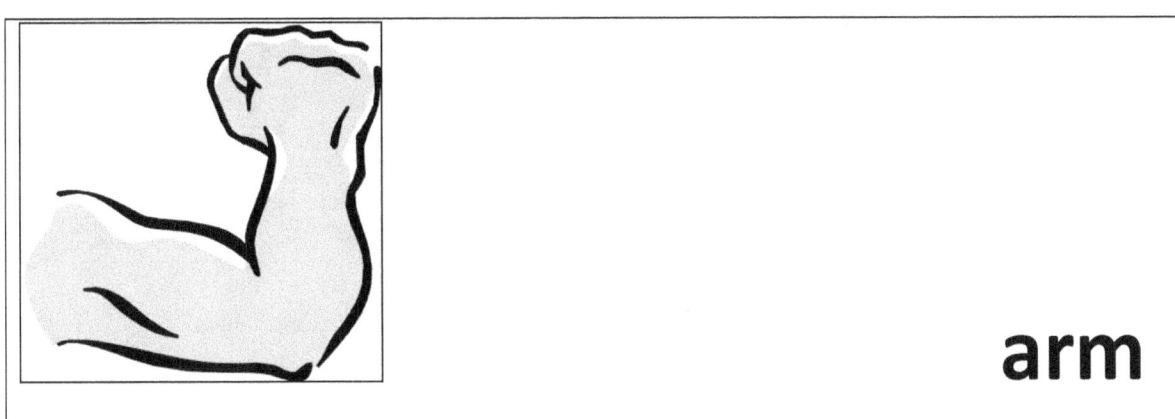 arm

 ears

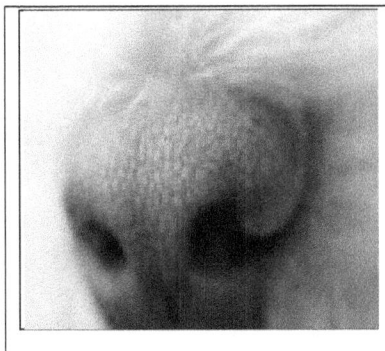 nose

"A New Home for Honey" Kindergarten – 1st grade
Vocabulary Cards

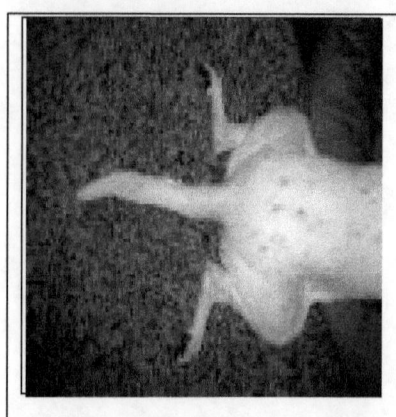 tail

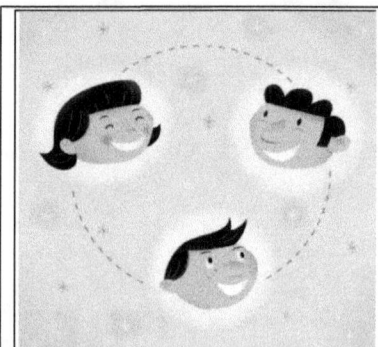 face

 dog body

"A New Home for Honey" Kindergarten – 1ˢᵗ grade
Vocabulary Cards

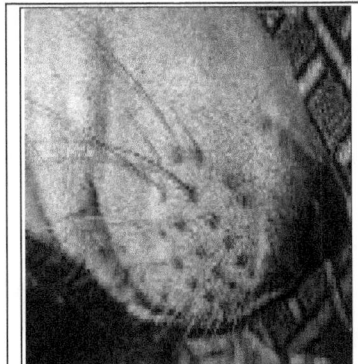 mouth and whiskers

Lesson 5: Honey's Peanut Butter Adventure - Math

Content Area: Mathematics

Grade Level: 1st

Learning Standards: estimate and measure length using nonstandard units such as paper clips, tiles, unifix cubes, etc.

Concepts: measurement, length, comparisons of lengths, comparative language, problem solving, answering questions

Time Frame: 40 minutes

MATERIALS AND RESOURCES:

1. *Honey's Peanut Butter Adventure* by Tom Greer
2. Paper or attached handout
3. Writing utensils (pencils, pens, markers, crayons)
4. 2-4 jars of peanut butter
5. 2-4 boxes of doggie treats (bone-shaped or any type that have length to them) or imitation treats made from construction paper
6. Paper clips or some other manipulative for non-standard measuring
7. Large floor space
8. Stuffed dog or construction paper made
9. 3 classroom chairs side by side to represent a couch

OBJECTIVES:

The students will be able to:

1. Estimate and measure length using non-standard units of measurement
2. Compare lengths

PRESENTATION/INTRODUCTION: attention getter

Students will be asked if they have a pet. If they do have a pet, ask them what kind of pet they have and to show how long their pet is by holding out their hands. Compare pet's lengths as this pet conversation continues. Example: Lily has a hamster and Henry has a dog. Which pet is longer?

Show the cover of the book and read the title, author and illustrator. Show the back of the book, spine of the book and its title page. Compare the cover and title page: are they the same or different? Re-read the title of the book, author and illustrator aloud.

Teacher reads "Honey's Peanut Butter Adventure" by Tom Greer. During the read aloud, the teacher should ask questions or say things such as "I wonder how far away the kitchen was from the couch?" or "I wonder how many rolls it took Honey to get the peanut butter from the kitchen to the couch?" and "I wonder what we could use to measure that?"

INTEREST BUILDING: why it is important

Ask students if they have ever wondered if something was longer in length than something else or how far away something is? For example, have you ever wondered if it is a longer walk to the library or to the office from the classroom? How would you answer that question? A: By measuring the length.

Look at the pages of the book where Honey is walking from the couch to the kitchen and rolling the peanut butter back to the couch. Discuss with the students whether or not they thought it was far from the couch to the kitchen. Have them think about how far their couch is from their kitchen.

CONTENT DEVELOPMENT: modeling/guided practice

1. Set up:
   Teacher takes 3 chairs and sits them side by side: this is a representation of the couch Honey was sitting on. Place stuffed dog-Honey on the couch.
2. The teacher then places 4 jars of peanut butter different distances away from the couch. This is the distance to be measured and may be moved closer or further away to add variety for groups.
3. Define length: the distance along something from end to end, or a measurement taken of this distance. As teacher reads or says this definition he/she should point from the couch to the peanut butter to add context clues.
4. Divide the students into 4 groups or more (if more, then teacher will need more jars of peanut butter) depending on class size.
5. Ask students each group to estimate how many paper clips and doggie treats they think it is going to take to get from the couch to the peanut butter. Teacher writes down each group's predictions on sheet provided to share with the class: one sheet per group for teacher writing.
6. Have each group measure and record their answers on their own sheet provided by teacher. Each group will measure the length to a different peanut butter jar in the room.
7. Once this is done, share each group's results and compare to their earlier predictions.
8. Teacher or student can demonstrate how to roll the peanut butter jar with his/her nose. Demonstrate one roll and two rolls. Now, ask each group to estimate in paper clips and doggie treats how far one roll will go. Teacher writes down their answers on sheet provided.
9. Have each group choose one member to be "Honey" and roll the peanut butter jar with his/her nose. Measure this roll from starting point to ending point using paper clips and doggie treats.
10. Once this is done, share each group's results and compare with earlier predictions.

SUMMARY/CLOSURE: review

1. The teacher will explain to the class that the activity they just did in groups they will do on their own.
2. Each student is given another sheet provided and a writing utensil in order to work independently.
3. They are to choose a different jar of peanut butter to measure the length from the couch.
4. They are to also to take turns rolling the jar of peanut butter once, then measure and record the length. Repeat this same step with two rolls.

5. As a bonus, they may count how many rolls it takes to get the jar of peanut butter back to the couch. They may write their answer on the back of their sheet.

EVALUATION: assess

1. After each student finishes, ask a couple of students to volunteer and demonstrate what they did when they were working on their own.
2. While in a large group each student's experiences and results.
3. As results are being read aloud, have them compare those with their own: "Did any one have the same results in any of the measurements?"
4. Ask: "What else could we have used to measure the length?"
5. "What other parts of our body could we use to roll the jar of peanut butter?"
6. If time permits: with the teacher, in small group, have the student measure different lengths with other non-standard units of measurement.

EXTENSION: center and homework

- Place peanut butter jars in center with different manipulatives for non-standard measurement

1. Roll the jar with different parts of your body i.e. nose, like Honey, hand, foot, elbow, etc.
2. Measure and record results
3. Compare lengths
4. See how far the jars will roll with different numbers of rolls.

- Teacher can base choices on what to measure in the student's home.

Measure the length from one place to the other in your home.

Example: from kitchen to living room, from bathroom to bedroom, from front door to back door from television to couch or from the couch to the kitchen just like Honey.

Items to use for non-standard measurement at home: feet, shoes, DVDs, cans of food, pencils, and utensils.

"Honey's Peanut Butter Adventure" 1st grade: Measuring Lesson
Teacher writes group predictions & groups use for activity

1. Measure the length from the couch to the peanut butter.	2. Roll with nose ONCE and measure the length.	3. Roll with nose TWICE and measure the length.
What is the length in paper clips? _____	*What is the length in paper clips?* _____	*What is the length in paper clips?* _____
What is the length in doggie treats? _____	*What is the length in doggie treats?* _____	*What is the length in doggie treats?* _____

53

Lesson 6: Honey's Peanut Butter Adventure – Language Arts and Social Studies

Content Area: Writing, Listening, Social Studies, History

Grade Level: Kindergarten – 1st grade

Learning Standards: recording knowledge of a topic, responding through talk & movement, reflect interpretation, problem-solving, decision making, perception of location

Concepts: inquiry/research, literary response, using problem solving to identify and solve a problem, use position terms to identify location.

Time Frame: 40 minutes

MATERIALS AND RESOURCES:

1. *Honey's Peanut Butter Adventure* by Tom C. Greer
2. Attached handout: dog pieces, kitchen items, position word cards
3. Writing utensils (pencils, pens, markers, crayons)
4. Students my bring a stuffed dog or other stuffed animal or some can be offered by the teacher
5. Housekeeping items: sink, table, chair, shelf, jar of peanut butter, stove
6. If housekeeping items are not available, use classroom furniture to represent the kitchen furniture

OBJECTIVES:

The students will be able to…
1. Record his/her own knowledge of a topic in various ways such as by drawing and showing connections among ideas
2. Respond through talk and movement to a story and reflect understanding and interpretation
3. Use the problem-solving process to identify a problem, gather information, list and consider options, consider advantages and disadvantages, choose and implement a solution and evaluate the effectiveness of the solution.
4. Use terms, including over, under, near, far, top, bottom, around, above to describe relative location.

PRESENTATION/INTRODUCTION: attention getter

Students will be asked to sit holding their stuffed animal. The students will be asked to put the animal on top of their head, under their foot, make it go around your arm, place your animal near you, now far away from you, etc. During this activity, the teacher should model the movements and positions the stuffed animal should be in. Have the students put their animals in their laps or behind them (teacher preference). Tell the students that Honey, the dog in the story, will have to move all around the kitchen to get her favorite treat. Let's see if it was easy for her to get to it or if it was hard for her to get to. Let's also see what did Honey had to do to get it?

Show the cover of the book and read the title, author and illustrator. Show the back of the book, spine of the book and its title page. Compare the cover and title page: are they the same or different? Re-read the title of the book, author and illustrator aloud.

Teacher reads "Honey's Peanut Butter Adventure" by Tom C. Greer. During the read aloud, the teacher should as questions or say things such as "What do you think Honey is going to have to do to get to the peanut butter first? Now what do you think she is going to do? Do you think she'll really get the peanut butter? Does Honey seem to be happy? Was it worth all the work to get the peanut butter?"

INTEREST BUILDING: why it is important

Ask students if they have ever had to find something? Teacher says, "Now when you were looking for it did you have to do a lot of thing to reach it? For example, did you have to walk over the rug, go under the doorway or maybe under the table to get what you wanted?" Allow students to share some stories and ask questions using specific positions words they used in their process.

Look at the pages of the book where Honey is in the kitchen trying to reach the peanut butter. Review all the things Honey had to do to get to the peanut butter. For example, Honey was on top of the chair, went around the sink and had to get to the bottom shelf on the counter to reach the peanut butter. Have them vote whether or not they thought it was easy or hard for Honey to reach the peanut butter and why they think so.

CONTENT DEVELOPMENT: modeling/guided practice

1. Set up: Teacher sets out housekeeping or classroom furniture to represent Honey's kitchen.
2. Teacher then shows position word cards and picture cards.
3. The teacher then demonstrates how to choose one card from each pile (positions and picture).
4. The cards will determine how to manipulate the stuffed animal i.e. over the sink, on the bottom of the stove, near the shelf, etc.
5. The teacher then performs a few sequences of choosing cards and manipulating the stuffed animal to match.
6. Choose students to come up and perform the same task.
7. After everyone has had an opportunity to manipulate their stuffed animal to match the position cards have them put their animal to the side.
8. The teacher asks the students to think about all the things Honey had to do to reach the peanut butter. Go through the book and have one or two students re-enact the entire scene with their stuffed animal.

9. The teacher then repositions the furniture in the "kitchen" and asks the students if they think it will be easier or harder now? What are all the things the stuffed animals will have to do to reach the peanut butter on the shelf?
10. Have a few students demonstrate what their stuffed animal would have to do to reach the peanut butter. Remind them to use the position words.
11. Have the students vote on whether moving the furniture made it harder or easier for the stuffed animal.
12. Reposition the furniture again and review the process steps 9 to 11.
13. Place the students in groups of 4 with their stuffed animals.
14. Each group will then be given a set of picture cards and position word cards to use.
15. Once this is done, the students are to take turns choose a card from each pile until everyone has had a chance and performed what is asked on the word card. The picture card now becomes the piece of furniture.
16. Upon completion of this activity, have the students choose three cards from each pile. These cards will help the group determine what set up of the furniture would be easiest for one of their stuffed animals to get to the peanut butter.

SUMMARY/CLOSURE: review

1. The teacher asks all the groups to come together and perform what they believe would be the easiest way for their stuffed animal to get to the peanut butter.
2. They are to show the other students the three cards that they chose from each pile and manipulate the furniture as they see fit.
3. One person from the group then has the stuffed animals perform the task at hand.
4. All groups share their choices, thoughts and ideas. Ask these questions: Why did they choose those words and furniture, did they find out they had to move things around, do you was it hard or easy for your stuffed animal?

EVALUATION: assess

1. The students may now go to their desks/tables and draw picture of what their group's stuffed animal just did.
2. Have word cards and picture cards available for students to document their results.
3. Once everyone is done, these pictures may be shared whole group, small group and/or placed in book form for the classroom library.
4. Small groups may be called to manipulate position words and document what they did.

EXTENSION: center and homework

- Place "Honey's Peanut Butter Adventure" in the handwriting center.
1. Make up your own story of how Honey got the peanut butter.
2. Answer: What would you do to make it really easy for Honey to get the peanut butter?

- Design your own kitchen in the block center/large foam blocks/ large legos and draw a picture.
- Manipulate dolls around the kitchen in housekeeping using position words.
- Leave position word cards and picture cards in a doll house center for students to use with smaller manipulatives.

- Teacher can ask parents to have students perform simple tasks such as:

    1. Put the book under the table.
    2. Throw the ball over the toy.
    3. Go near the front door.
    4. Stand far away from me.
    5. Etc.

"Honey's Peanut Butter Adventure" K - 1st grade Position cards
Student chooses dog to manipulate and move to different positions: over, under, etc.
Teacher cuts out pictures of kitchen furniture items and position word cards to use.

"Honey's Peanut Butter Adventure" K - 1st grade Position cards
Student chooses dog to manipulate and move to different positions: over, under, etc.
Teacher cuts out pictures of kitchen furniture items and position word cards to use.

"Honey's Peanut Butter Adventure" K - 1st grade Position cards
Student chooses dog to manipulate and move to different positions: over, under, etc.
Teacher cuts out pictures of kitchen furniture items and position word cards to use.

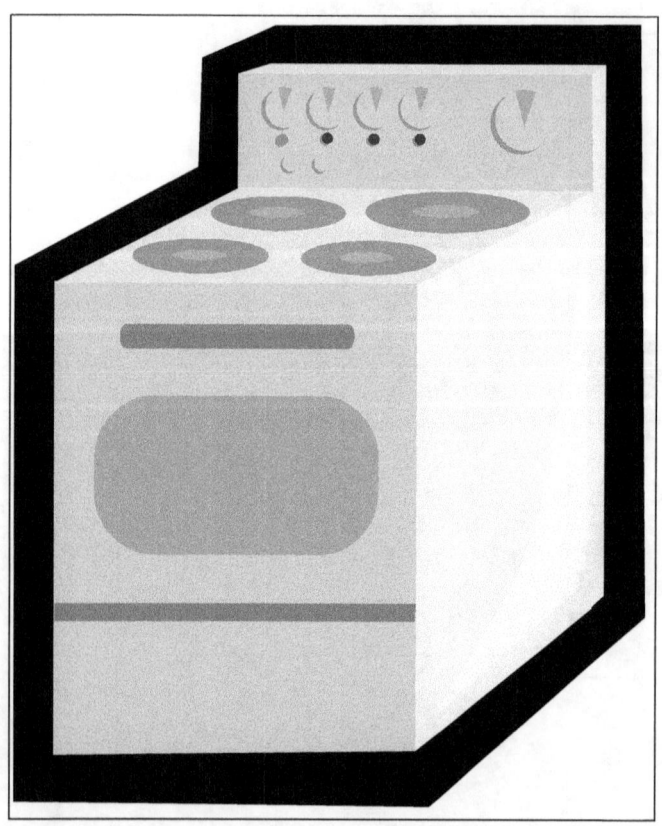

"Honey's Peanut Butter Adventure" K - 1st grade Position cards
Student chooses dog to manipulate and move to different positions: over, under, etc.
Teacher cuts out pictures of kitchen furniture items and position word cards to use.

"Honey's Peanut Butter Adventure" K - 1st grade Position cards
Student chooses dog to manipulate and move to different positions: over, under, etc.
Teacher cuts out pictures of kitchen furniture items and position word cards to use.

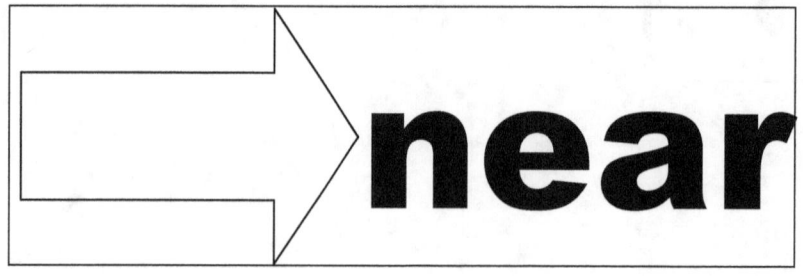

"Honey's Peanut Butter Adventure" K - 1st grade Position cards
Student chooses dog to manipulate and move to different positions: over, under, etc.
Teacher cuts out pictures of kitchen furniture items and position word cards to use.

Lesson 7: Honey's Peanut Butter Adventure – Language Arts and Geography

Content Area: Geography, Listening, Reading, Writing

Grade Level: 2nd

Learning Standards: simple geographic tools/maps, writing, read fluently, listening, speaking

Concepts: maps, oral reading, write for purpose, listen for purpose, present story

Time Frame: 40 minutes

MATERIALS AND RESOURCES:

1. *Honey's Peanut Butter Adventure* by Tom Greer
2. Attached handouts: black and white maps
3. Additional maps than those provided (if desired)
4. Large chart paper for a list and to draw a map of Honey's kitchen
5. Blank paper to write story on
6. Writing utensils (pencils, pens, markers, crayons)

OBJECTIVES:

The students will be able to…
1. Draw a map to show places
2. Write a story
3. Read orally from familiar text with fluency, accuracy and expression
4. Participate in discussions
5. Present dramatic interpretation of story

PRESENTATION/INTRODUCTION: attention getter

Teacher will display a variety of maps. Ask the students, "Who knows what theses are? What is it used for? Why would anyone want a map? What kinds of maps do you have? Are there any in your car or house? Do you know what they are used for? Have you ever seen these sort of maps (attached sheet of maps) before? These are maps the inside of houses. Now let's look at the inside of this dog's house (point to Honey), her name is Honey. In this story, Honey moves all around her kitchen to get her favorite treat. Let' see where it's at and how she gets to it.'

Show the cover of the book and read the title, author and illustrator. Show the back of the book, spine of the book and its title page. Compare the cover and title page: are they the same or different? Re-read the title of the book, author and illustrator aloud.

Teacher reads "Honey's Peanut Butter Adventure" by Tom Greer. During the read aloud, the teacher should ask what room was the treat in and point out all the moves Honey is doing to get to the peanut butter such as jumping from the chair and walking on the counter. Upon completion, review the pages where Honey is moving all around the kitchen and name all the furniture pieces, appliances and maneuvers Honey was doing to get to the special treat.

INTEREST BUILDING: why it is important

Show students pictures of room maps attached with this lesson. Explain that these maps are maps of rooms and not maps of countries, cities or states. Have the students take a good look at the map then try and name the rooms and/or the items located in the rooms. Review all the maps in detail by describing shapes and what different things represent.

Look at the pages of the book where Honey is in the kitchen. Tell them we will now draw a map of Honey's kitchen that will look similar to these room maps.

CONTENT DEVELOPMENT: modeling/guided practice

1. Set up: Have students come up one to the large chart paper one at a time to write down a list. This list should contain all of the pieces of furniture or appliances we will need to draw a map of Honey's kitchen.
2. Once the list is complete, tear it from the chart paper tablet and hang it nearby.
3. Open the book and look at the kitchen picture. Review the list and make sure the list is complete.
4. The teacher now begins to draw the map. Have the students offer suggestions and shapes to use to represent all the items in Honey's kitchen.
5. One this map is complete, review it. Have a few students come up to the room and label or simply name the items represented in the map.
6. Other students could demonstrate how Honey had to move around the kitchen in order to get her treat with the use of the map.
7. Now to go a bit further, have the students get into pairs and come up with another way Honey could move through the kitchen to get to the treat.
8. Once the plan is decided upon, have the pairs come up and explain.
9. Hold a discussion on any similar routes and ideas students may have had in common.

SUMMARY/CLOSURE: review

1. Ask the students why they think we would want a map of a room.
2. Give each student two sheets of blank paper: one for a map and one for the story.
3. The teacher will explain to the class that they will now design their own kitchen or room where Honey will have to find a treat. This map is what Honey will be able to use to find the treat.
4. Explain to the students that we will create map design of a room. They will use this map to help write a story telling us how Honey can get to the treat.
5. Each student is given a story writing sheet and blank sheet of paper to draw map of their room.

EVALUATION: assess

1. Once the student finish, they will come up one at a time to present their maps and stories.

2. Before the students begin their presentations the rest of the students will try to decipher the map by guessing which room it is and what located in the room.
3. While in a large group each, the student will share their map and story.
4. Once everyone has participated, compare rooms to check for similarities and differences. For example, compare two kitchen and two living rooms.
5. Ask students what they learned about maps or drawing maps.
6. Ask students: Was it hard to read a map of a room before? Is it easier now? If you could design another room which would it be and what would it have in it?

EXTENSION: center and homework

- Place die cuts of circles, square rectangles, etc in a center where students can manipulate them on a large sheet of construction paper in order to design a room.
- Have students draw a map of their classroom.
- Write a story about your pet getting into his/her favorite treat.

- Homework: Draw a map of your bedroom or draw a map of your house or dream house.

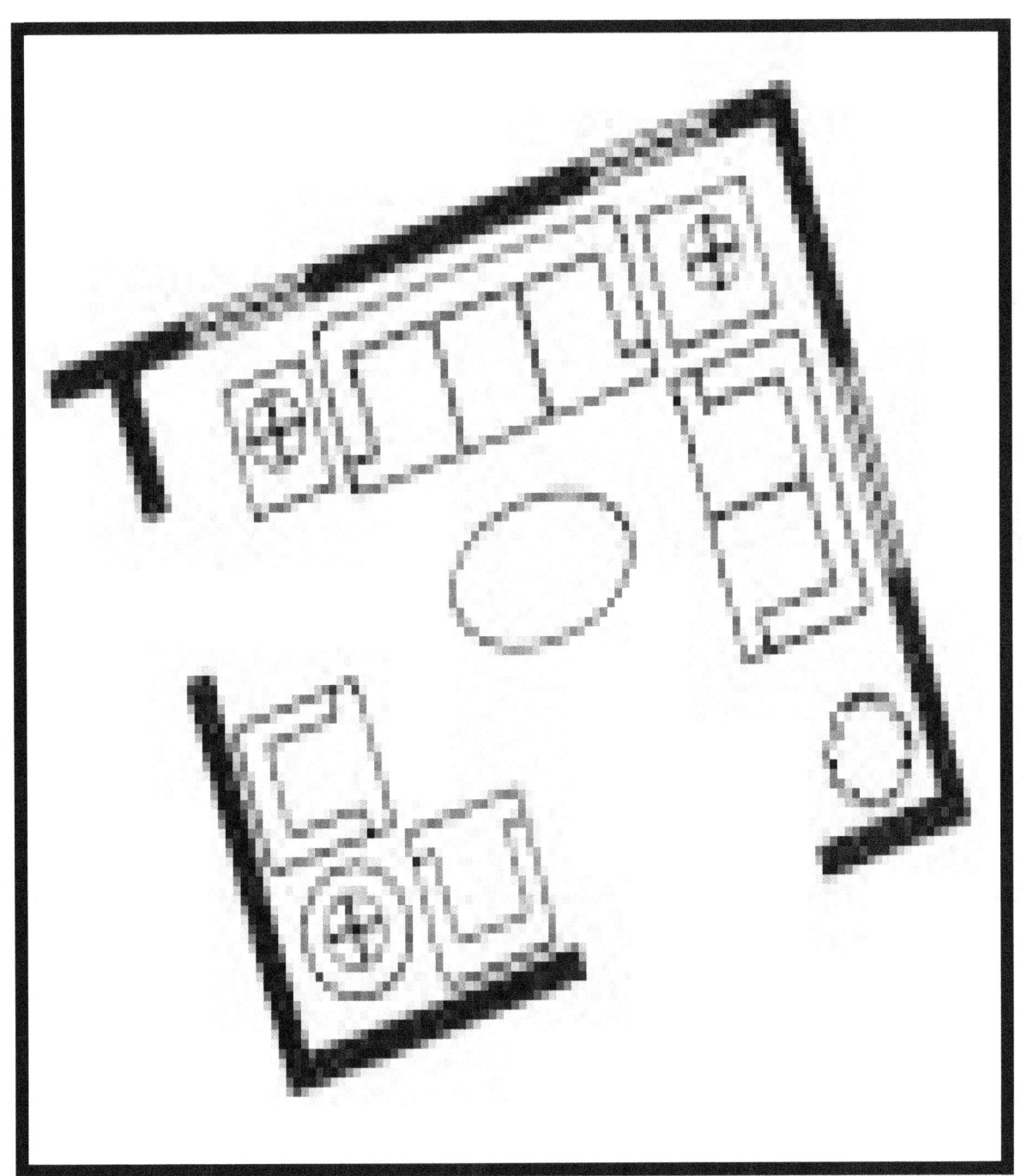

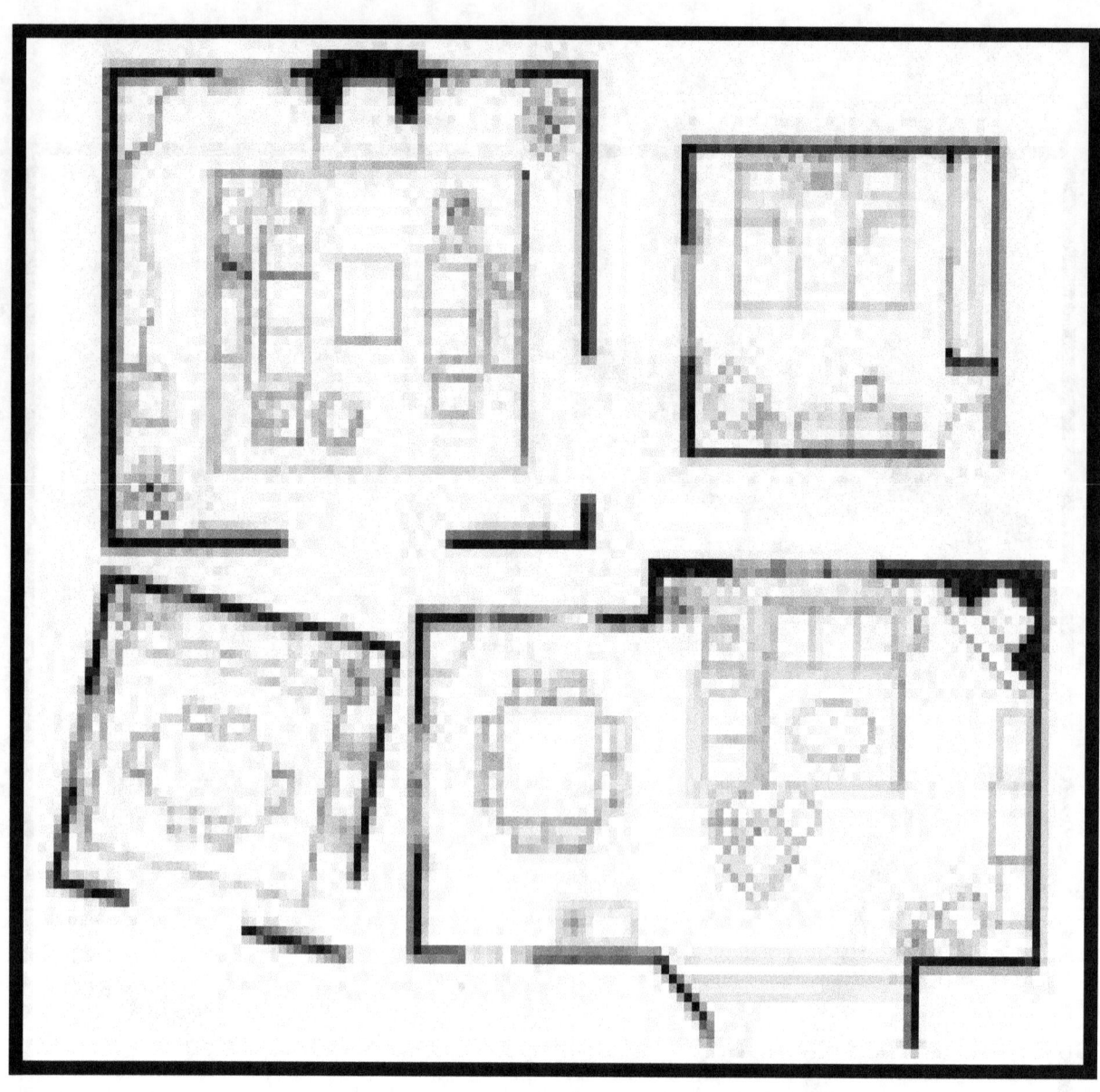

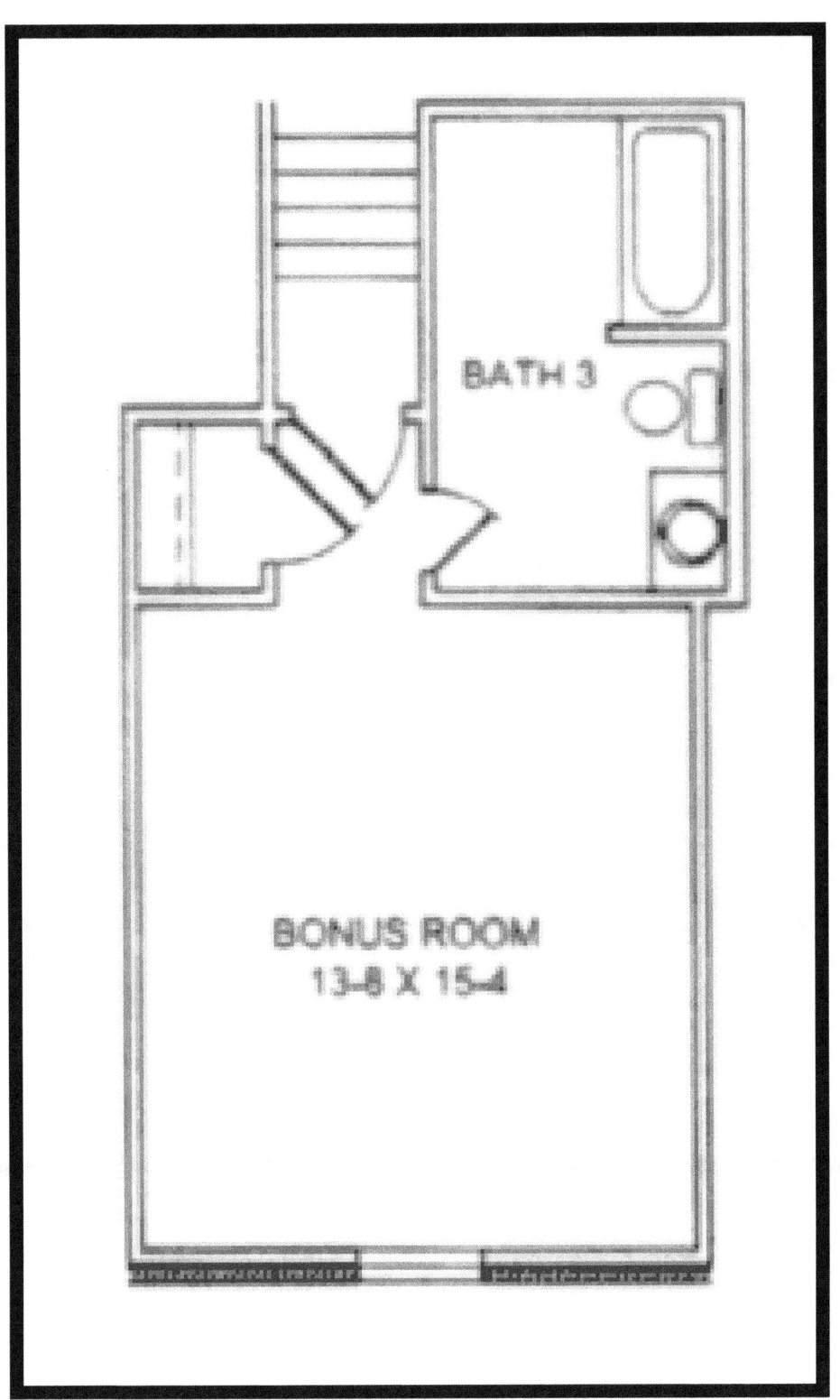

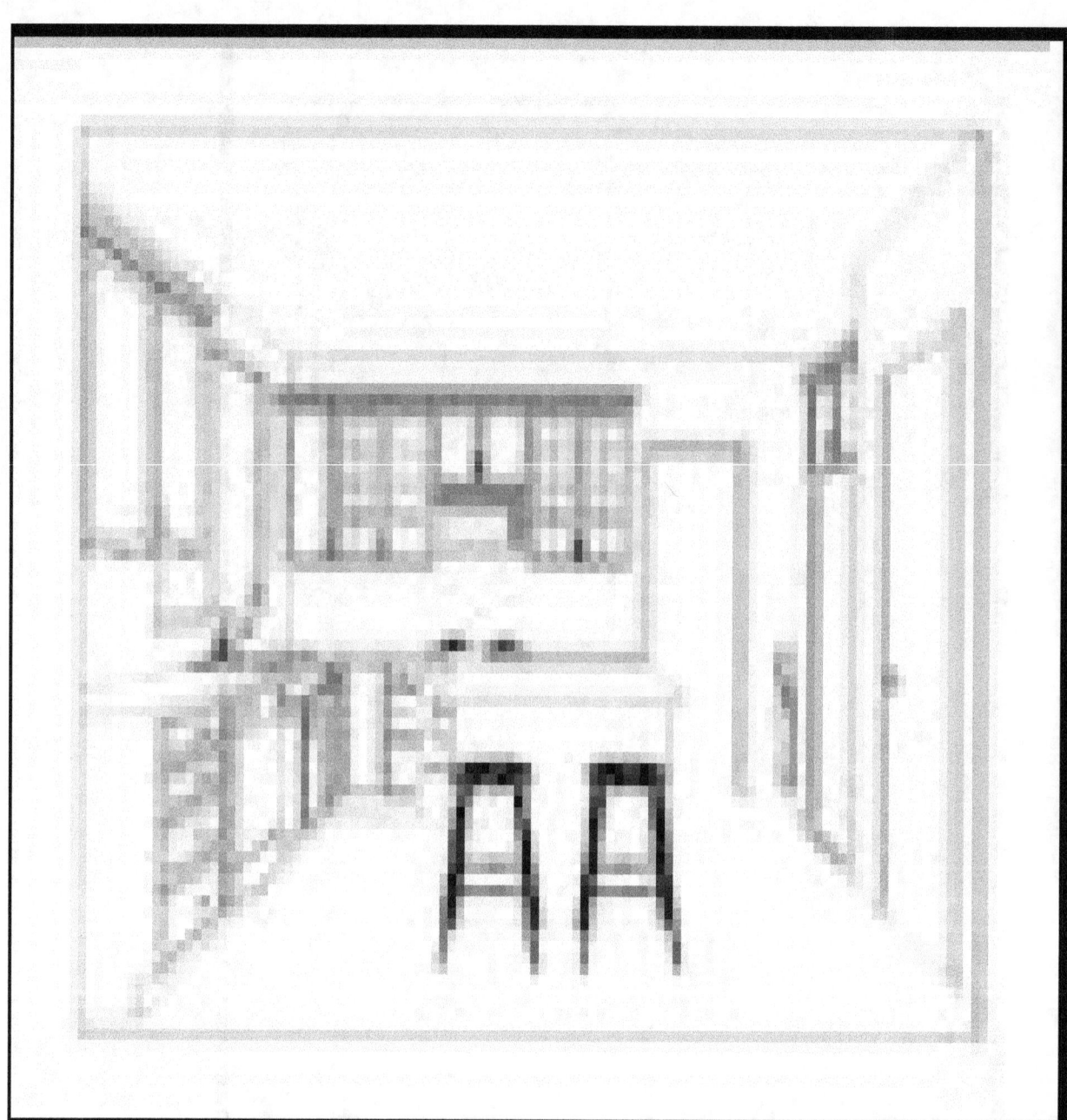

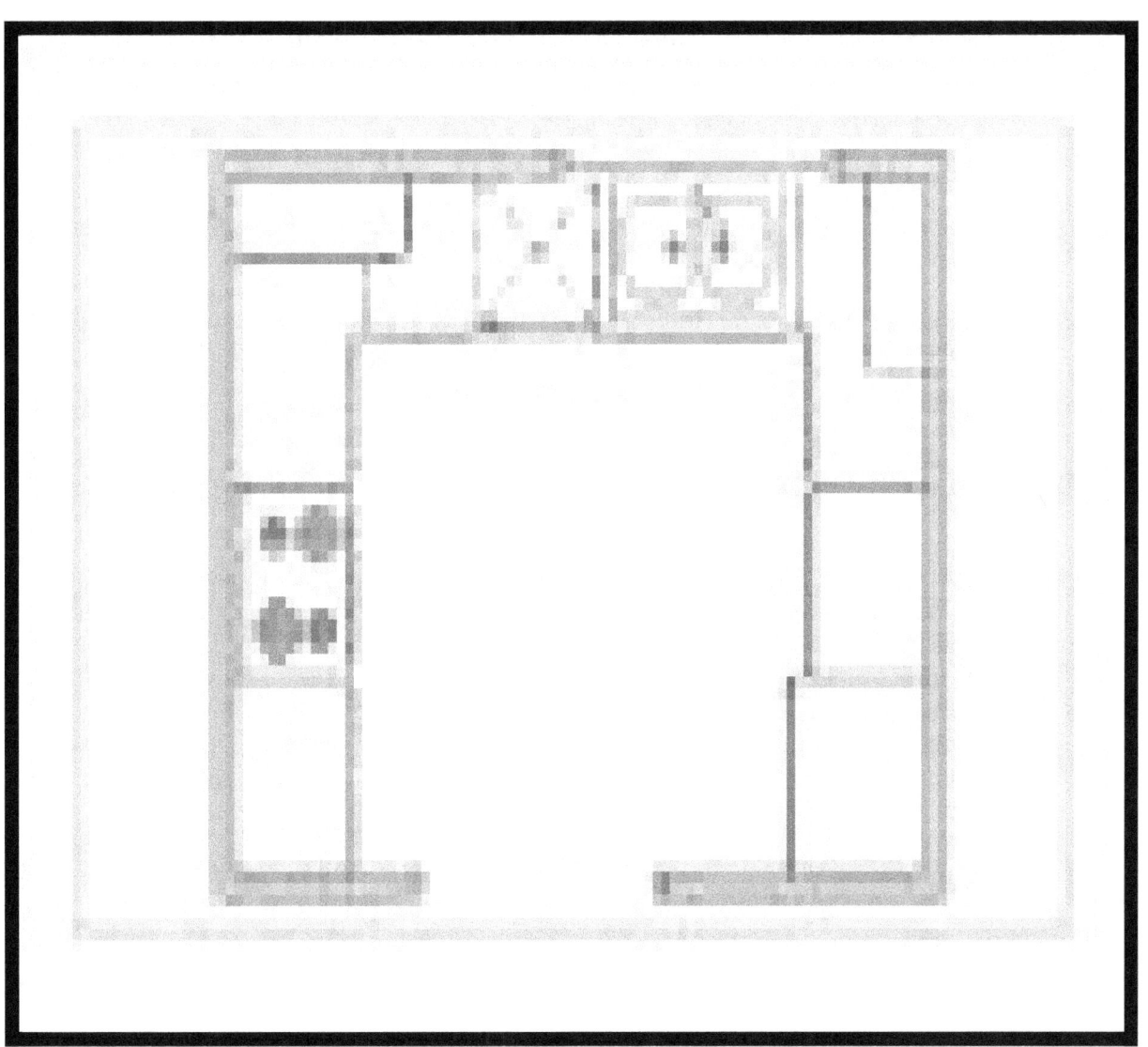

Lesson 8: Honey's Peanut Butter Adventure – Math and Science

Content Area: Mathematics/Science

Grade Level: 1st

Learning Standards: sort objects according to their characteristics, use whole numbers to describe and compare quantities

Concepts: food pyramid (fruits and vegetables), constructing picture graphs, comparing numbers

Time Frame: 40 minutes

MATERIALS AND RESOURCES:

1. *Honey's Peanut Butter Adventure* by Tom Greer
2. Attached handouts: Large vegetable/fruit sorting cards: one copy for teacher
    vocabulary word cards: one set for graph (students will place picture card underneath word card)
    sorting and graph titles: one copy for teacher
    small pictures for picture graph: one picture card per student
    graphing class results sheet: one per student
3. Large poster or picture of the food pyramid (not absolutely necessary but can be used as a reference)
4. Writing utensils (pencils, pens, markers, crayons)
5. 1 – 2 jars of peanut butter
6. Apples
7. Pears
8. Bananas
9. Celery
10. Lettuce
11. Carrots
12. Paper plates
13. Napkins

OBJECTIVES:

The students will be able to...
1. Distinguish between fruits and vegetables
2. Categorize and sort fruits and vegetables
3. Construct a picture graph
4. Compare whole numbers to determine less than, greater than or equal to using a pictorial model

PRESENTATION/INTRODUCTION: attention getter

Students will be shown a basket of whole fruits and vegetables that the teacher has prepared. The teacher asks "Who likes to each any of these foods? Do you know the names of them?" Allow students to respond and name as many as they can. The teacher should hold up the food item as it is being named. Once all the food items in the basket are named, ask the students if they like to eat these types of foods as a snack? Remind the students that all these foods are healthy snacks unlike donuts, chips and candy. Now, cut each type of food in half and show the inside. Have the students pass the cut up fruits and vegetables. Have the students smell and feel these food items. Hold a little discussion on how each item tastes and who whether or not they like it. Put the cut up food and basket of other food away. Tell them you are going to read them a story about Honey the dog who gets to eat her favorite treat. Tell the students that at the end of the story you are going to ask them what her favorite treat was and whether or not you like it too.

Show the cover of the book and read the title, author and illustrator. Show the back of the book, spine of the book and its title page. Compare the cover and title page: are they the same or different? Re-read the title of the book, author and illustrator aloud.

Teacher reads "Honey's Peanut Butter Adventure" by Tom Greer. During the read aloud, the teacher should as questions or say things such as "Do you like peanut butter? I wonder if it's crunchy or smooth peanut butter? I wonder if she likes peanut butter on other foods like fruits and vegetables." At the end of the story ask, "What was Honey's favorite treat? How many of you like peanut butter? Have you ever eaten it with fruits or vegetables?" At this time, the teacher should bring the basket of food back out.

INTEREST BUILDING: why it is important

At this time, lay out the large picture cards and vocabulary cards naming fruits and vegetables. Ask students if they know which of these foods are fruits and which are vegetables? Direct the children to the food pyramid and show them where each of these categories fits in. Hold up a few items and see if the students guess correctly. Begin taking out one food item at a time and have the students guess whether it is a fruit or vegetable. Then place the food item in front of the correct picture card. Once all the food is sorted, name the items in each group. Ask the students if they thought any of the foods was suppose to be in the other category and which food.

Have the students discuss which of these foods they have tasted before and which they have never tasted. Tell the students that they will get to taste each of the fruits and vegetables today. Some students may be reluctant to try these foods. Do your best to make the foods enticing and appealing.

The teacher may cut up all of the fruits at this time and all of the vegetables: it would be a great idea to have parents pre-cut the items for you but make sure to save some whole foods for the beginning of the lesson.

Ask the students to sort the food items on their plates by fruits and vegetables. As a whole group, taste each food item on the plate one at a time. At the end of the tasting have the students choose one of their favorite of the fruits and of the vegetables. The students may take part in the pictorial graph at this time. Place the title "Which fruit and vegetable did you like best?" at the top of the graph. The students will then choose the corresponding picture cards to their favorite choices and participate in the graphing exercise. Review the results of the graph: how many liked each item? Where there any items no-one liked? Which fruit did the students like the most, less and least? Which vegetable did the students like the most, less and least?

Look at the pages of the book where Honey is enjoying her favorite treat of peanut butter on the couch. Discuss with the students that they will now try the fruit and vegetable of their choice with peanut butter.

CONTENT DEVELOPMENT: modeling/guided practice

1. Set up:
   Teacher gives children a spoonful of peanut butter, a piece of their favorite fruit and a piece of their favorite snack.
2. The students will now dip their fruit item into the peanut butter and taste it.
3. The students will then dip their vegetable item into the peanut butter and taste it.
4. Ask the students to decide which of the two items they tasted did they like best with Honey's favorite treat, peanut butter.
5. The students will participate in another pictorial graph but this time choosing one item of the two to represent their favorite overall choice. The title for this graph is "Which food tastes best with peanut butter?" The students will use little picture cards to represent their choice.
6. Review the results of this graph by counting the choices for each food item.
7. Discuss which fruit tasted best and which was liked least with peanut butter according to the graph results.
8. Discuss which vegetable tasted best and which was liked least with peanut butter according to the graph results.
9. Look at the pictorial graph again and see which food category was liked best with peanut butter overall. Was it the vegetable or the fruit category?

SUMMARY/CLOSURE: review

1. Show the students the graphing class results sheet and demonstrate how to record the class results. Give the students the option of writing the numerical answer on their answer sheet.
2. The students will now be given a graphing sheet. They are to record the class graphing results.
3. They are to draw pictures in the boxes to represent each picture on the graph.
4. This activity is to be done independently.
5. Remind them that this sheet represents what we decided at a class through our tasting activity.
6. Have the students review which food item was like the most in each category and the least from each category.

EVALUATION: **assess**

1. After each student finishes, re-group.
2. While in a large group each student's experiences while making the pictorial graph. Did they find it easy or hard to do? What was easy? What was hard?
3. Go through their answer sheets, with the help of the large pictorial graph they used to record their results and check their answers.
4. Ask the students, "What other fruits or vegetables could we have used to try with peanut butter? Do you think they would have tasted good?"
5. "Were any of you surprised to find out that your favorite fruit or vegetable tasted good with peanut butter?"

EXTENSION: **center and homework**

- Place fruits and vegetables in a center. (pictures, real or plastic food items)

1. Sort the food items into fruit and vegetable categories.
2. Make a real object graph of fruits and vegetables in this center. Record your results. Which had the most? Which had the least?
3. Paint your favorite fruits and vegetables.
4. Paint with fruits and vegetables.

- For homework:

1. Make a list of all the fruits and vegetables your family likes to eat.
2. Take home an empty graph like the one used in this activity and graph which of these fruits and vegetables your family likes best.

"Honey's Peanut Butter Adventure" Food Groups and Graphing Pieces
Large cards are for sorting.
Vocabulary picture and word cards are for sorting and graphing.
Small fruit and vegetable pieces are for choosing favorite and graphing.

"Honey's Peanut Butter Adventure" Food Groups and Graphing Pieces
Large cards are for sorting.
Vocabulary picture and word cards are for sorting and graphing.
Small fruit and vegetable pieces are for choosing favorite and graphing.

 **Fruits**

 **Vegetables**

 **apple**

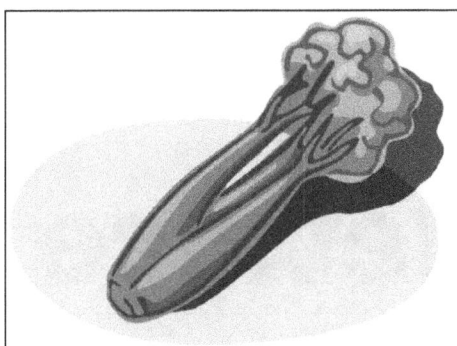 **celery**

"Honey's Peanut Butter Adventure" Food Groups and Graphing Pieces
Large cards are for sorting.
Vocabulary picture and word cards are for sorting and graphing.
Small fruit and vegetable pieces are for choosing favorite and graphing.

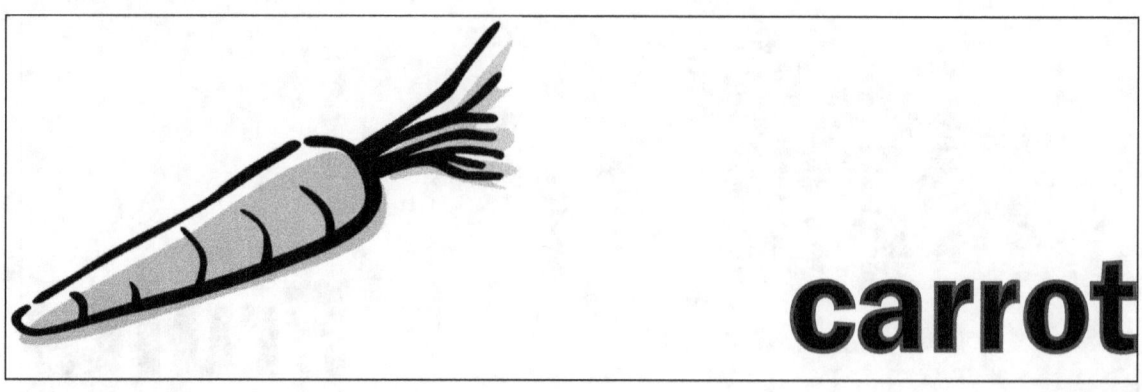

carrot

banana

pear

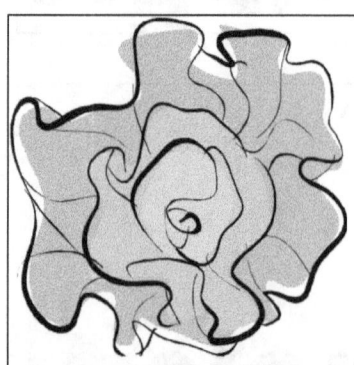

lettuce

"Honey's Peanut Butter Adventure" Food Groups and Graphing Pieces
Large cards are for sorting.
Vocabulary picture and word cards are for sorting and graphing.
Small fruit and vegetable pieces are for choosing favorite and graphing.

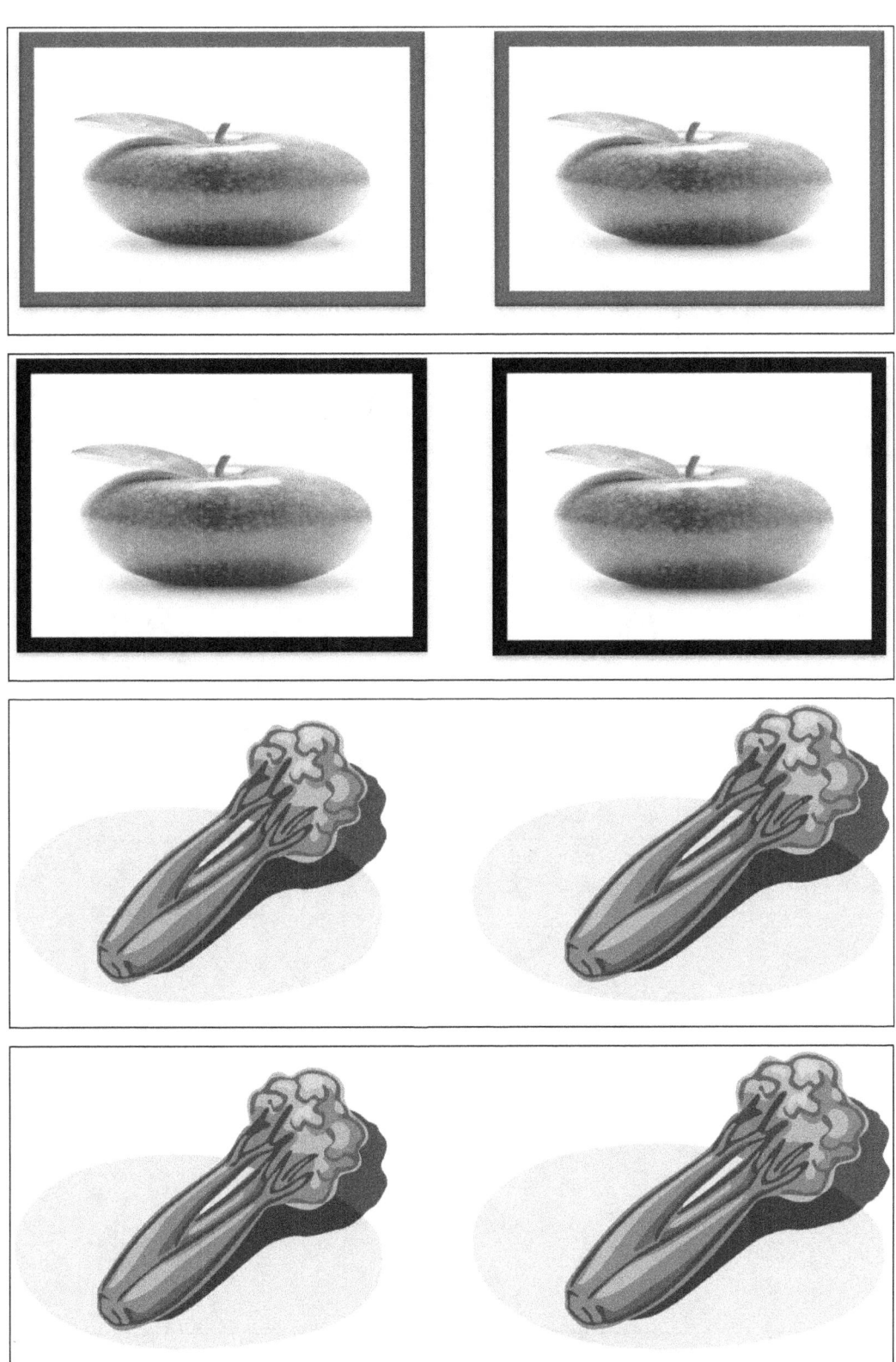

"Honey's Peanut Butter Adventure" Food Groups and Graphing Pieces
Large cards are for sorting.
Vocabulary picture and word cards are for sorting and graphing.
Small fruit and vegetable pieces are for choosing favorite and graphing.

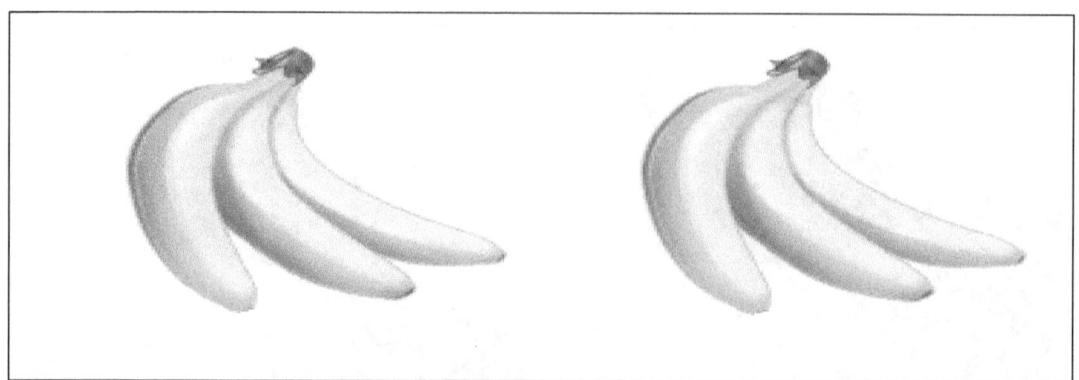

"Honey's Peanut Butter Adventure" Food Groups and Graphing Pieces
Large cards are for sorting.
Vocabulary picture and word cards are for sorting and graphing.
Small fruit and vegetable pieces are for choosing favorite and graphing.

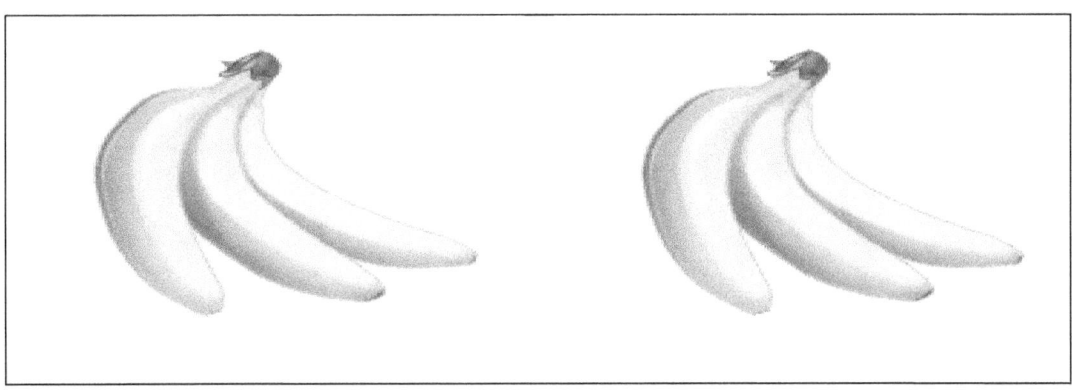

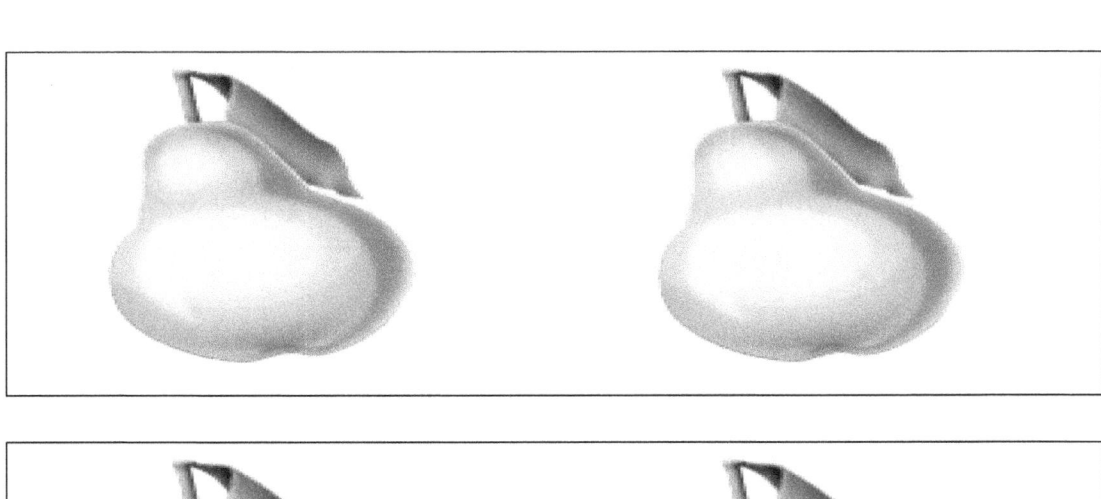

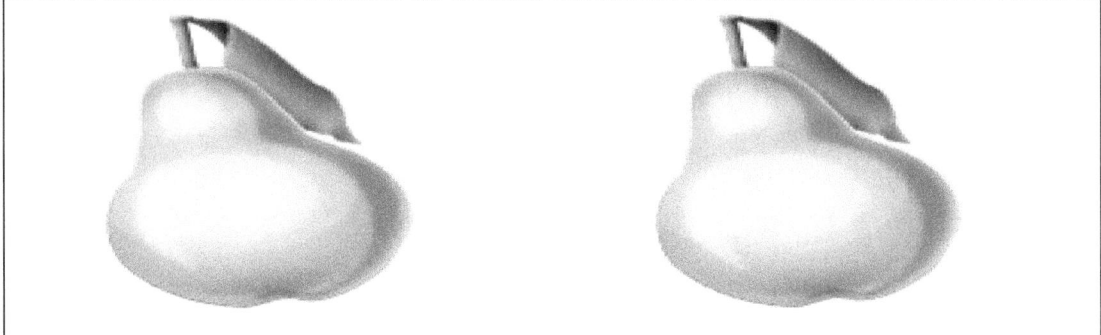

"Honey's Peanut Butter Adventure" Food Groups and Graphing Pieces
Large cards are for sorting.
Vocabulary picture and word cards are for sorting and graphing.
Small fruit and vegetable pieces are for choosing favorite and graphing.

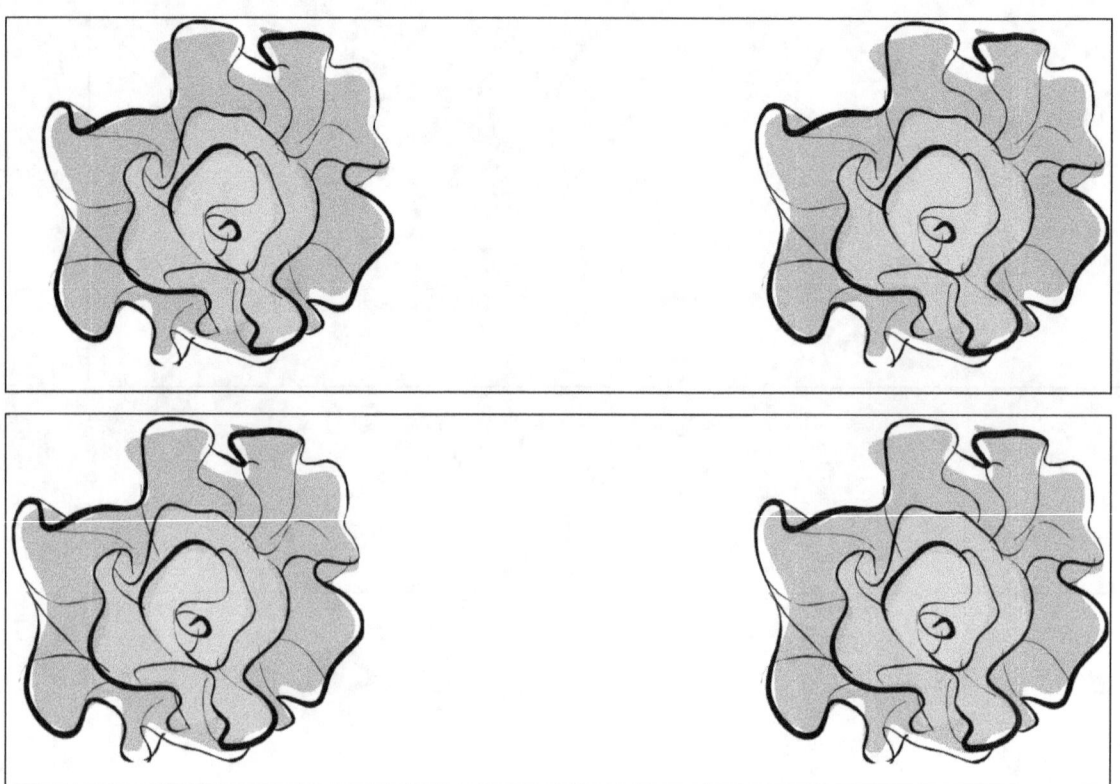

"Honey's Peanut Butter Adventure" 1st grade Mathematics & Science
Graphing sheet for Favorite Fruits and Vegetables with Peanut Butter
Students draw food item in each box to represent the class choice results.

apple	banana	pear	celery	carrot	lettuce

Our class results:

Which food item tasted best with peanut butter?

Sort the fruits and vegetables

Which food tastes best with peanut butter?

Which fruit and vegetable did you like best?

Lesson 9: Honey Visits Grandpa Smith – Math

Content Area: Mathematics

Grade Level: Kindergarten – 1st

Learning Standards: identify, describe and extend pictorial and concrete patterns

Concepts: use repeating patterns and additive patterns to make predictions, a-b-c pattern

Time Frame: 40 minutes

MATERIALS AND RESOURCES:

1. *Honey Visits Grandpa Smith* by Tom Greer
2. Large chart paper
3. Writing utensils/markers
4. Paper or attached handout: pattern cards (3 cards per set) each pair of students will need at least 2 sets, pattern worksheet (1 per student)
5. Scissors
6. Glue
7. Pattern blocks, manipulatives to build patterns, unifix cubes

OBJECTIVES:

The students will be able to…
1. Identify an a-b-c pictorial and concrete pattern
2. Describe an a-b-c pictorial and concrete pattern
3. Extend an a-b-c pictorial and concrete pattern
4. Create pictorial pattern (homework)

PRESENTATION/INTRODUCTION: attention getter

Students will be asked if they know what a pattern is. Allow students to discuss? Teacher defines the term pattern: it is something that is repeated; it is predictable and can be used as a model or design. Tell the students they are found everywhere in life: music, clothing, life cycles, pictures, etc. Ask them if they remember seeing or hearing any patterns before.

Show the cover of the book and read the title, author and illustrator. Show the back of the book, spine of the book and its title page. Compare the cover and title page: are they the same or different? Re-read the title of the book, author and illustrator aloud.

Teacher reads "Honey Visits Grandpa Smith" by Tom Greer. After the reading, go through the pages and name some items that would be good to use to make patterns. Be sure to name some of the items on the pattern cards attached. Also, make sure the cards are already cut up and ready to use. The teacher will place the students into pairs or a small group at this time. The students will need at least two copies of each set in order to create an a-b-c pattern: once repeated. As a whole group, make a-b-c patterns with the picture cards provided. Have the students switch off their sets of cards in order to create a different a-b-c pattern. Do this procedure a few times.

To go a step further, combine sets and extend the a-b-c pattern a few times and allow the students to participate in this process. Allow them to predict what will come next and manipulate the pattern themselves. Be sure and make mistakes while participating in the building and extending of the pattern so the students may correct them.

INTEREST BUILDING: **why it is important**

At this time have the students put the pattern cards away. Ask the students to think of where we might find patterns in the world. Ask them why they think there are patterns and why they are be important.

Tell the students you will be showing them a pattern and they are to repeat it. The teacher will then clap some sort of pattern with his/her hands and the students are to repeat it. The teacher can now repeat the process with stomping or some other body movements. If there is music available with a definite pattern repeated that could be used as well. The teacher can then point out any patterns on clothing, any located within the classroom or around the school. Discuss with the students what type of pattern it is they are looking at.

Hold a small discussion on the importance of patterns in our world. Tell them there are patterns in music just like we played with our hands or listened to with our ears. Remind them of those we see in the classroom. Discuss patterns in the life cycle of humans and animals: if available show life cycle cards of baby to adult. Tell the students patterns help us know what is going to happen or come next.

. **CONTENT DEVELOPMENT:** **modeling/guided practice**

1. Tell the students they will be put into pairs.
2. The teacher will pass out manipulatives for the students to use. They will use the manipulatives to build different patterns.
3. Once every group has their manipulatives, the teacher can begin by laying out a pattern for the children to copy. For example blue-red-yellow.
4. The students will copy the pattern and then attempt to extend the pattern a full set.
5. Repeat this a-b-c pattern process a few times. Then allow the pairs to create their own a-b-c pattern and share with the class.
6. At this time put the manipulatives away and get out the large chart paper.
7. Use markers to draw different patterns such as circle-square-triangle or sun-moon-star and have the students come up and complete the patterns by drawing what comes next. If drawing is not desired, die-cut pictures work well, too.
8. Once everyone has had a chance to draw a section of a pattern put away the writing/drawing utensils.

SUMMARY/CLOSURE: review

1. Have a few students come up to the front of the class and read the patterns that were drawn on the large chart paper. Allow the other students to chime in and continue saying the pattern even past the visuals.
2. Ask again where patterns are found and why they are important.

EVALUATION: assess

1. The students will be given the attached worksheet: What comes next?
2. They will need scissors and glue for this activity.
3. Once everyone has completed their sheets, review them.
4. In a small group, the teacher may use pattern cards or manipulatives to have students, copy, create and extend a-b-c patterns.

EXTENSION: center

- Place different sets of die cuts in center for students to create patterns. Perhaps have pre-made pattern sheets for students to copy and extend.
- Make pattern cards for students to lay manipulatives on top of and/or extend.
- Have a variety of manipulative available for pattern building.
- Place pattern cards in music center for students to play on instruments.
- Have patterns of music available for listening.

- Homework:

- create an a-b-c pattern and draw it out
- List 5 patterns you find in your home
- Did you see any patterns outside? Did you hear any patterns on the radio or on TV?

"Honey Visits Grandpa Smith" Kindergarten – 1st
Complete the a-b-c pattern worksheets

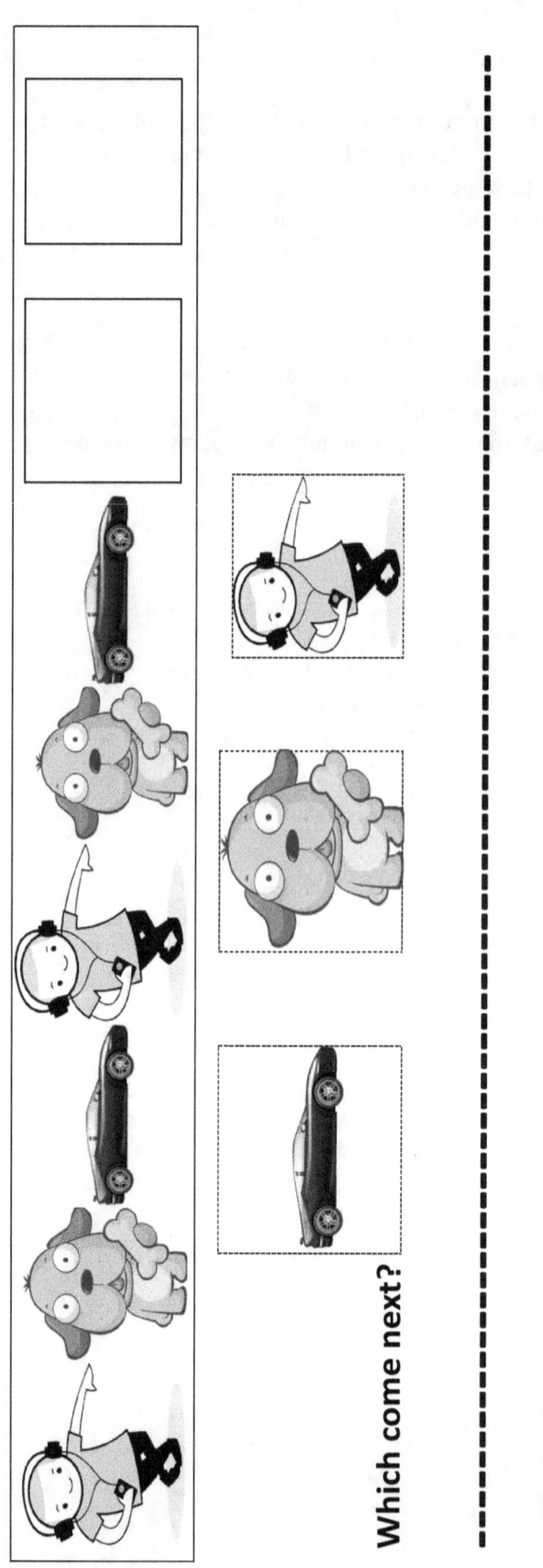

Which come next?

Which come next?

"Honey Visits Grandpa Smith" Kindergarten – 1st
Complete the a-b-c pattern worksheets

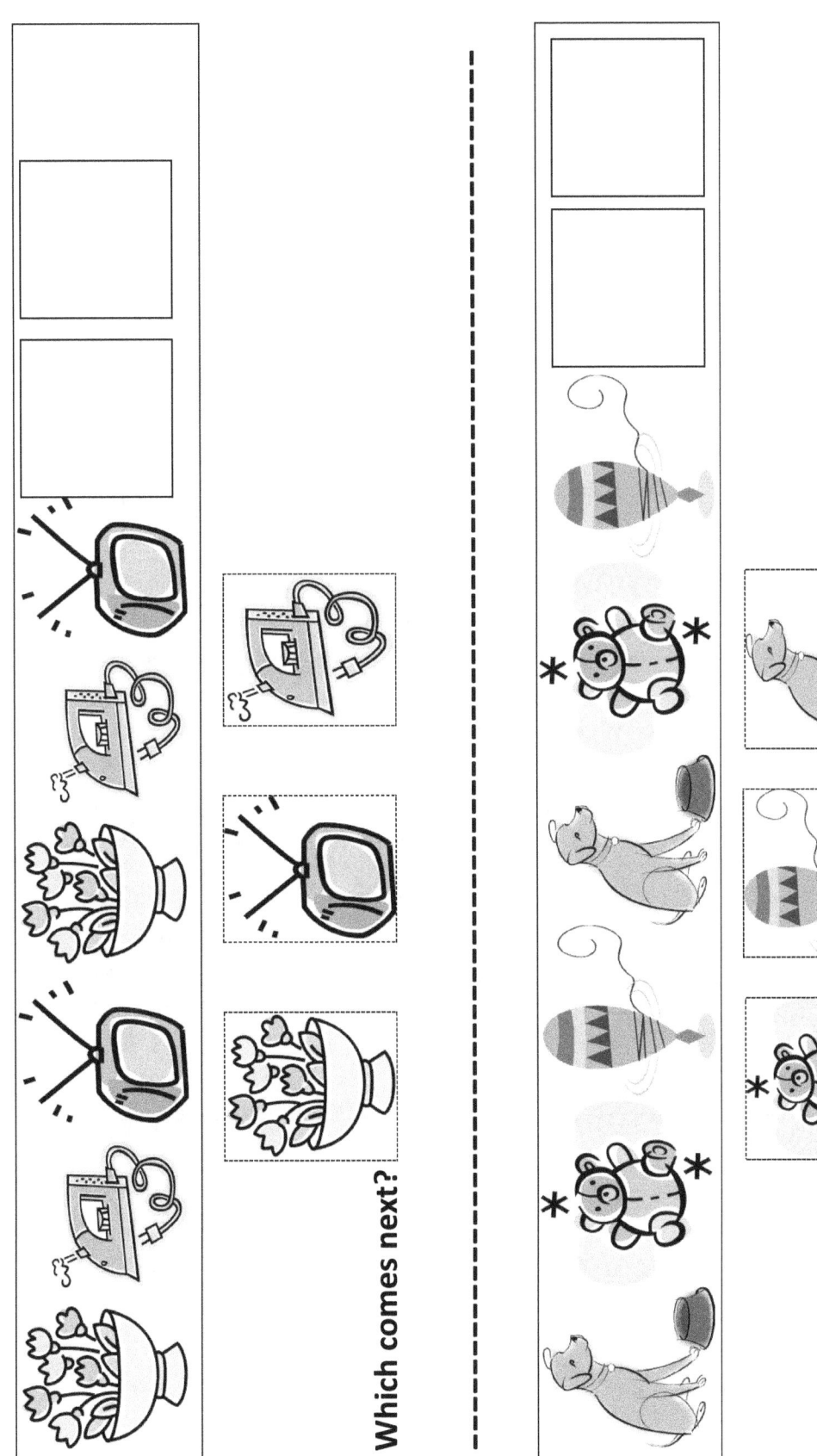

Which comes next?

Which comes next?

"Honey Visits Grandpa Smith" Kindergarten – 1st
Pattern cards: a-b-c pattern cards
Dog house-people house-teepee
Dog-boy-grandpa
Mixer-blender-toaster
Teddy-dog-bone
Knife-fork-spoon

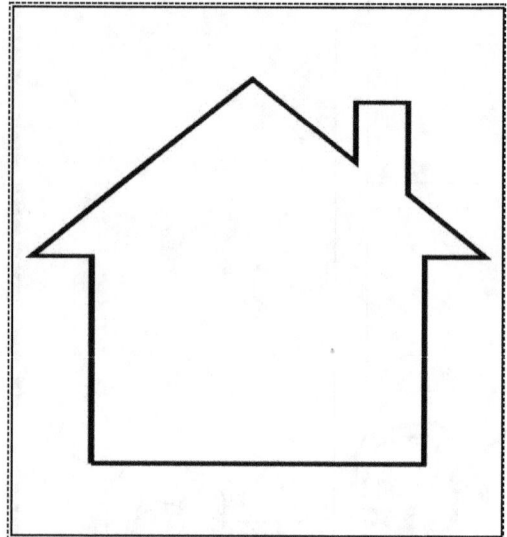

"Honey Visits Grandpa Smith" Kindergarten – 1st
Pattern cards: a-b-c pattern cards
Dog house-people house-teepee
Dog-boy-grandpa
Mixer-blender-toaster
Teddy-dog-bone
Knife-fork-spoon

"Honey Visits Grandpa Smith" Kindergarten – 1st
Pattern cards: a-b-c pattern cards
Dog house-people house-teepee
Dog-boy-grandpa
Mixer-blender-toaster
Teddy-dog-bone
Knife-fork-spoon

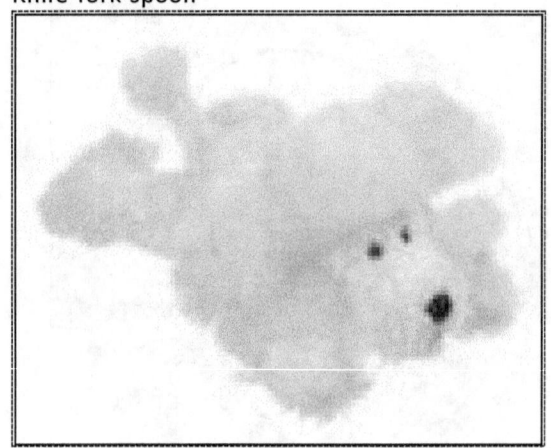
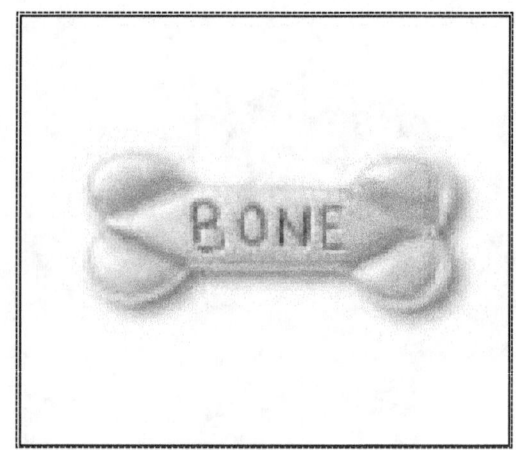
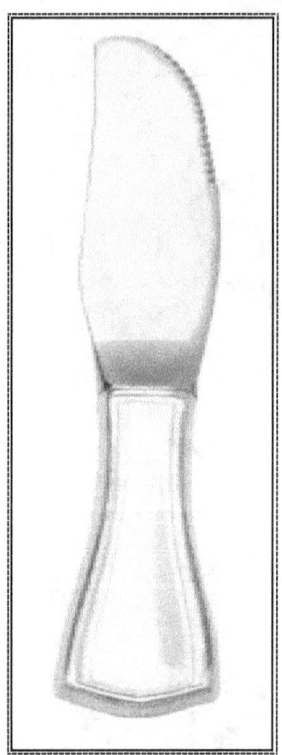
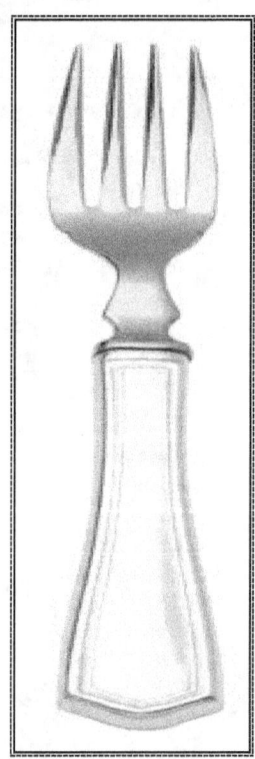

Lesson 10: Honey Visits Grandpa Smith – Math

Content Area: Mathematics

Grade Level: Kindergarten

Learning Standards: use concrete objects to represent quantities in written form

use numbers to describe how many objects are in a set

use verbal and symbolic descriptions to describe how many

use sets of pictorial objects to compare whole numbers

Concepts: uses numbers to name quantities, uses whole numbers to describe and compare quantities

Time Frame: 40 minutes

MATERIALS AND RESOURCES:

1. *Honey Visits Grandpa Smith* by Tom Greer (and extra copies if available or students can share)
2. Number cards 0-20
3. Large foam dice or teacher made
4. Small dice for students (while in pairs)
5. Writing utensils/markers
6. Paper or attached handouts: bingo cards, pair and independent worksheets
7. Scissors
8. Glue
9. Manipulatives or die cuts or felt board pieces or beans (anything the children can use to count and represent values)

OBJECTIVES:

The students will be able to…
1. Identify use objects to represent quantities
2. Use numbers to describe "how many" in a set
3. Read and write numerals 0-12
4. Compare quantities of whole numbers

PRESENTATION/INTRODUCTION: attention getter

Students will be asked if they know how to count. As a group, count from 0 to 10 or 20 aloud. Now show students number cards and see if they know the names of the numbers. The teacher can then hold up fingers and see if they know the value. Count different things in the room, for example, count how many red shirts, how many boys and/or girls are in the classroom.

Show the cover of the book and read the title, author and illustrator. Show the back of the book, spine of the book and its title page. Compare the cover and title page: are they the same or different? Re-read the title of the book, author and illustrator aloud.

Teacher reads "Honey Visits Grandpa Smith" by Tom Greer. During the reading, be sure to count some of the items in the pictures like people, doors, windows, etc. The teacher should focus on pages with lots of items to count. Once an item is counted, have the students hold up the corresponding value with their fingers. After the reading, this process could be repeated with a few more items while going through the pages.

INTEREST BUILDING: **why it is important**

Ask the students why they think it is important to know about numbers? Why is it important to know what they look like or how much a number is worth? Ask them where do we find numbers in the world? Where are there numbers in the classroom? Where can we find numbers in our homes? Show students number cards and tell them each number has a name and each number has its own value.

At this time pass out bingo cards and bingo markers to the students. The teacher should demonstrate how to play the game. The cards will all get filled at the same time> the object of the game is to match the numbers and fill up your card. The teacher may then begin the game by calling out one number at a time. The teacher should make sure to walk around and verify the student's number recognition.

Have the students switch cards and repeat the game. Perhaps this time a student can take turns calling out the numbers. Once the games are complete have the students put away their bingo cards and bingo markers. Discuss if the students were having any difficulty recognizing any of the numbers. Review and share which numbers they were.

CONTENT DEVELOPMENT: modeling/guided practice

1. Tell the students to sit in a circle.
2. The teacher will pass out manipulatives for the students to use. They will use the manipulatives to build numbers rolled out on the dice.
3. At this time the teacher can demonstrate how to throw the dice and then build the number.
4. Allow the students to each have a turn throwing the dice while everyone builds each number rolled.
5. Once everyone has had a chance to roll the dice and build numbers, repeat the process with two dice in order to build larger numbers.
6. Put the students into pairs and have them repeat the procedure: one rolls the dice and the other builds the number.
7. Students can now put away their manipulatives and dice.
8. The pairs will need the attached sheet where they will be writing the number values and answering one question.
9. They will also need writing utensils.

10. The students will go through the book or copies of the pictures that coincide with the worksheet and answer the questions.

SUMMARY/CLOSURE: review

1. Once all the pairs have completed their worksheet, review and compare their answers.
2. Have the students count aloud from 0 to 10 or 20.
3. Show the students number cards and have them say the number and show the value with their fingers.
4. Have the students discuss why numbers are important?
5. Ask the students why we should know how to read and write numbers?
6. Also ask, "What could happen if we didn't know how to read numbers?"

EVALUATION: assess

1. The students will be given a different attached worksheet to go through the book and work from.
2. Students can also write and build numbers using manipulatives.
3. In a small group, the teacher may roll a dice and have students build numbers or match number words to values. The teacher may even ask which has less or more.

EXTENSION: center

- Place different sets of die cuts, manipulatives, felt board pieces in center for students to count. Perhaps have large or small dice available for the students to throw and build numbers.
- Have number cards for students to lay manipulatives on top or under to build number values.
- Have number puzzles available.
- Lay number bingo cards in center for continued use.
- Match number word to value to numeral cards. (Teacher can make these)
- Number Bingo
- Lay out number lines and have students place manipulatives on top of number or build the value next to the number.

- Homework:

- Count the number of doors in your home.

- How many windows are in your home?

- How many sinks do you have?

- Do you have more tables or chairs?

"Honey Visits Grandpa Smith" Kindergarten – 1st
Mathematics: Number Bingo

10	5	6 ..... .
3 ...		2 ..
0	4	8 ....
1 .	9	7 ....

"Honey Visits Grandpa Smith" Kindergarten – 1st
Mathematics: Number Bingo

1 .	6	4 ....
10		8 ....
5	2 ..	0
7	3 ...	9 ....

"Honey Visits Grandpa Smith" Kindergarten – 1st
Mathematics: Number Bingo

1 ▪	9 ▪▪▪▪▪ ▪▪▪▪	3 ▪▪▪
6 ▪▪▪▪▪ ▪		7 ▪▪▪▪▪ ▪▪
4 ▪▪▪▪	8 ▪▪▪▪▪ ▪▪▪	2 ▪▪
10 ▪▪▪▪▪ ▪▪▪▪▪	5 ▪▪▪▪▪	0

"Honey Visits Grandpa Smith" Kindergarten – 1st
Mathematics: Number Bingo

3 ...	6	0
8		4 ....
1 .	10	7 ....
5	2 ..	9 ....

"Honey Visits Grandpa Smith" Kindergarten – 1st
Mathematics: Number Bingo

4	6	2 ..
8		9 ....
1 .	3 ...	5 .....
10	7	0

"Honey Visits Grandpa Smith" Kindergarten – 1st
Mathematics: Number Bingo

	These bingo cards can be placed on construction paper and laminated for durability.	

"Honey Visits Grandpa Smith" Kindergarten – 1st
Counting and writing in pairs activity

Pages 2-3

1. How many trees do you see?

2. How many stones are on the ground?

3. How many windows are on the house?

4. How many tires do you see?

5. How many letters are in the name "Smith?"

6. Which had the most?_____

"Honey Visits Grandpa Smith" Kindergarten – 1st
Counting and writing in pairs activity

Pages 4-5

1. How many trucks are there?

2. How many little buildings did Grandpa Smith have in his backyard?

3. How many boards were lying on the ground?

4. How many people were in the back yard?

5. How many barrels are there?

6. Which had the most? _____

"Honey Visits Grandpa Smith" Kindergarten – 1st
Counting and writing in pairs activity

Pages 7-8

1. How many televisions do you see?

2. How many vacuums do you see?

3. How many boxes are there?

4. How many blenders do you see?

5. How many tables are in the room?

6. Which had the most? _____

"Honey Visits Grandpa Smith" Kindergarten – 1st
Counting and writing in pairs activity

Pages 9-10

1. How many forks do you see?

2. How many telephones do you see?

3. How many things do you see have a plug?

4. How many can openers are there?

5. How many pots are there to cook with?

6. Which had the most? _____

"Honey Visits Grandpa Smith" Kindergarten – 1st
Counting and writing in pairs activity

Pages 15-16

1. How many chairs do you see? ☐

2. How many people do you see? ☐

3. How many eyes can you count? ☐

4. How many dogs are on page 15? ☐

5. How many puppy dog dolls did Honey find? ☐

6. Which had the most?_____

Lesson 11: Honey Visits Grandpa Smith - Math

Content Area: Mathematics

Grade Level: 1st - 2nd

Learning Standards: constructs picture graphs, draws conclusions, answers questions based on picture graphs, use data to describe events as more likely or less likely.

Concepts: interpreting information, probability and statistics

Time Frame: 40 minutes

MATERIALS AND RESOURCES:

1. *Honey Visits Grandpa Smith* by Tom Greer
2. Large chart paper for brainstorming and listing
3. Paper or attached handout: category cards (1 per group and 2 per student)
4. Paper or attached handout: 1 storage shed per group and 2 storage sheds per student
5. Paper or attached handout: Probability (1 per group and 2 per student)
6. Writing utensils (pencils, pens, markers, crayons)
7. Assorted kitchen items: real items or pictures
8. Assorted toys: real items or pictures
9. Large box for real items or small box for pictures
10. Sentence strips to write category titles on: kitchen items and toys
11. scissors

OBJECTIVES:

The students will be able to...
1. Organize data to make it useful for interpreting information
2. Sort pictures
3. Categorize pictures
4. Graph pictures
5. Describe whether a certain category was more or less likely to be chosen
6. Scribe probability

PRESENTATION/INTRODUCTION: attention getter

Students will be asked if they have ever been on an adventure. Have students share their adventure stories. Anyone go to the same places for the same types of adventures? The teacher can ask who has had a zoo adventure or a circus adventure. What types of things do you see there? Do you think you would see a clown on a space adventure or an elephant on an ocean adventure? Remind the students that there are certain things you would see in certain places and there are certain things you might want to know before you go on an adventure. Hold up the book and introduce Honey. Tell the children that she is about to go on an adventure herself.

Show the cover of the book and read the title, author and illustrator. Show the back of the book, spine of the book and its title page. Compare the cover and title page: are they the same or different? Re-read the title of the book, author and illustrator aloud.

Teacher reads "Honey Visits Grandpa Smith" by Tom Greer. During the read aloud, the teacher should as questions or say things such as "I wonder what sort of adventures Grandpa Smith has gone on?" or "I wonder if Honey likes her new adventure at Grandpa Smith's?" "What do you think?" "How can you tell?" Make comments about all the different items Grandpa Smith has in his storage from his different adventures.

INTEREST BUILDING: why it is important

Ask students to brainstorm a short list of different adventures they think Grandpa Smith may have gone on. Show the page in the book where Grandpa Smith, Tommy and Honey are standing in front of all the storage sheds. In the story, there were ten different storage sheds containing many different items from his adventures. Mention how it is important to keep things organized in order to find things easily. Go over the list and name some things Grandpa Smith may need on these adventures.

Look at the pages of the book where Honey is looking inside the storage shed at all the boxes. Discuss what may be inside those boxes and what sort of adventure that room may be about. Now turn to the pages with kitchen items and toys. Ask the students, "What could Grandpa Smith do if all his stuff was messed up?" A: Sort the items into the correct boxes and place them in the correct storage shed.

CONTENT DEVELOPMENT: modeling/guided practice

1. Tell the students they will be put into groups and will be able to choose from 2 adventures that they would like to go on BUT they have to pick the correct adventure card 4 times in order to go on the adventure.
2. The teacher places the students into 4 or more groups, depending on class size.
3. Each group is given a choice of adventure cards to choose from… or the teacher may just pass the adventure sheets out to his/her preference. Once the cards are passed out, have one student from the group cut out the cards.
4. Have students sort, categorize, and title the two types of adventures.
5. The adventure/category title that the group creates can be written on side of the storage shed.
6. Lay out the cards to make a pictoral graph, count and record the results on the Probablity answer sheet.
7. Make a choice of which adventure you or your group would like to go on.
8. Now, lay cards face down and you or someone from the group choose 4 cards… Out of those 4 cards, how many times did you choose the adventure you or your group wanted? Record your answers on your sheet.

9. Have students use their data/results to describe whether they were more or less likely to pick a card from a certain category/adventure.
10. Write down the probability and share.

SUMMARY/CLOSURE: review

1. Student or teacher, again define probability and how it is determined.
2. Students can discuss what they noticed as the game was played and how answers were recorded.
3. The teacher will explain to the class that the activity they just did in groups, they will do on their own.
4. Each student is given 2 more answer sheets and 2 storage sheds and writing utensil in order to work independently.
5. Students are to also choose 2 different sets of adventure cards to work with.

EVALUATION: assess

1. After each student finishes, ask a couple of students to volunteer and demonstrate what they did when they were working on their own.
2. While in a large group share each student's experiences and results.
3. As results are being read aloud, have them compare those with their own: "Did any one have the same results?" "What were the adventures you worked with?"
4. "How many of you would get to go on your adventure based on this game?"
5. Ask: "Why should probability matter to you?" "Why would we want to know if our chances are better at picking one thing over another?" In this case, you wanted to be able to go on a certain adventure.

EXTENSION: center

- Place different sets of adventure category cards out for students to sort, categorize by name, graph and determine probability. Also, place pictures of storage sheds: these may be laminated for durability, as well as the category cards.

1. Choose two different sets of category cards
2. Sort the cards onto the storage sheds
3. Name each category and write it down
4. Lay out category cards in graph fashion i.e. in a hanging chart graph, or from top to bottom or left to right on a table.
5. Choose an adventure from your cards that you would like to go on.
6. Turn the cards face down and choose 4...how many times did you choose the adventure you wanted?
7. Under each category: determine the probability and write it down
8. Write down whether each category was more or less likely to be chosen.

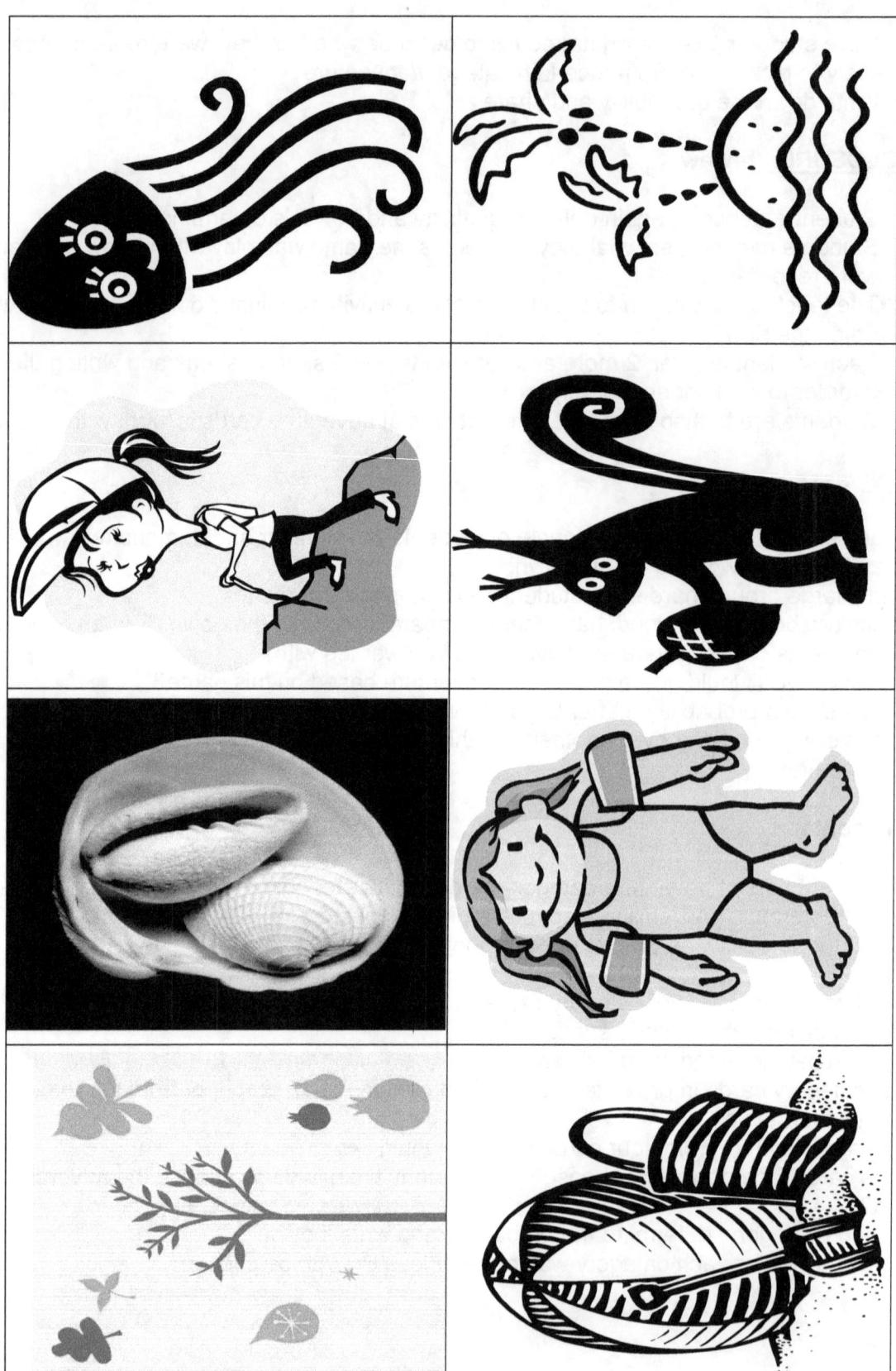

"Honey Visits Grandpa Smith" 1st-2nd grade Sorting, Graphing, Probability and Statistics

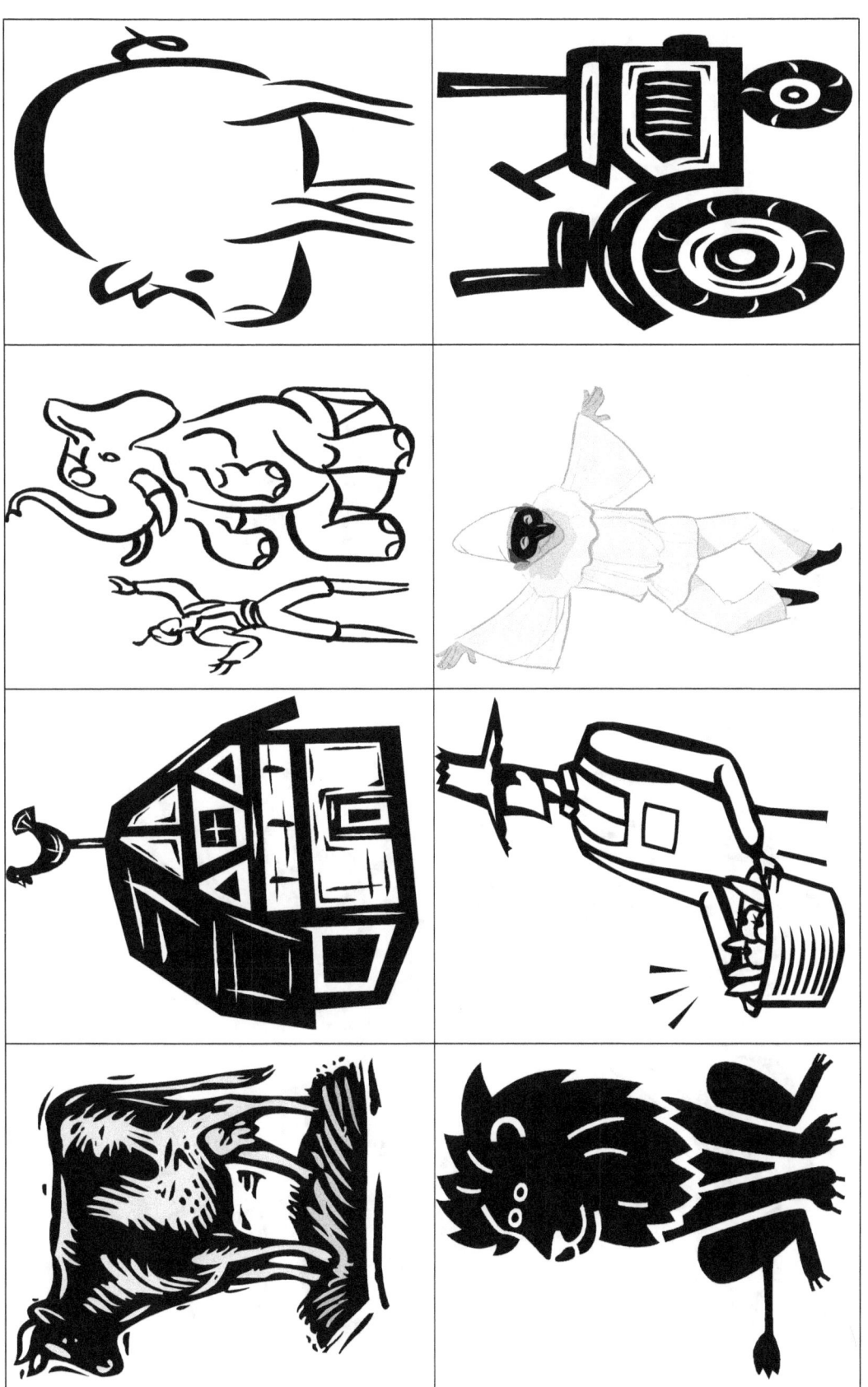

"Honey Visits Grandpa Smith" 1st-2nd grade Sorting, Graphing, Probability and Statistics

Adventure card categories	Copies you will need:	Directions:	
Set 1: Nature Walk and Beach Set 2: Farm and Circus Set 3: Rainy Day and Sunny Day Set 4: Dinosaur and Insect Set 5: Space and Park Set 6: Fire Station and Library	**Adventure cards** - 1 set per group - Independent work: 2 sets - Some can be placed in a center. **Storage sheds** - 2 storage per group - Independent work: 2 storage sheds - Some can be placed in a center. **Probability Sheets** - 1 set per group - Independent work: 2 sets - Some can be placed in a center.	1. Give each group a set of cards; they may be pre-cut or cut up by the group. 2. Have students sort, categorize, and name the two types of adventures. 3. The adventure/category title that the group comes creates can be written on side of the storage shed. 4. Lay out the cards and make a pictoral graph, count and record the results.	5. Make a choice of which adventure you would like to go on. 6. Now, lay cards face down and choose 4 cards...how many times did you choose the adventure you wanted? 7. Have students use their data/results to describe whether they were more or less likely to pick a card from a certain category/adventure. 8. Write down the probability and share.

Storage shed – 1 per group, 2 per student, some for a center

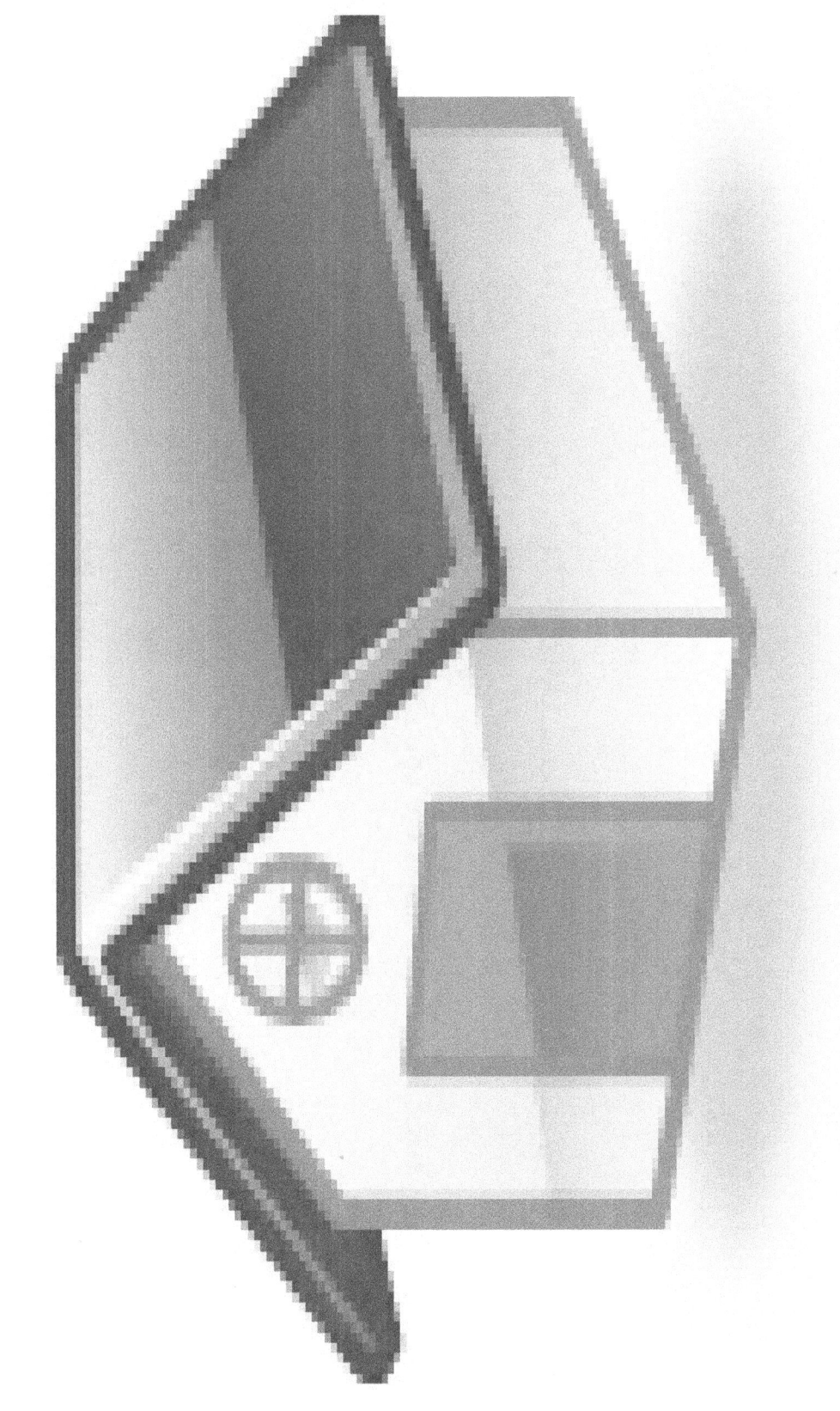

"Honey Visits Grandpa Smith" 1st-2nd grade Sorting, Graphing, Probability and Statistics

Probability Sheet: 1 per group, 1 per student, some for a center

- _____ out of _____ are a _____ adventure.

- _____ out of _____ are a _____ adventure.

1. Out of the 4 tries, how many times did you pick the adventure you or your group wanted? _____

2. Which adventure are you *more likely* to choose from the cards? _____

3. Which adventure are you *less likely* to choose from the cards? _____

4. Was it an EVEN chance?   Yes or No

"Honey Visits Grandpa Smith" 1st-2nd grade Sorting, Graphing, Probability and Statistics

Probability Sheet: 1 per group, 1 per student, some for a center

- _____ out of _____ are a _____ adventure.

- _____ out of _____ are a _____ adventure.

1. Out of the 4 tries, how many times did you pick the adventure you or your group wanted? _____

2. Which adventure are you *more likely* to choose from the cards? _____

3. Which adventure are you *less likely* to choose from the cards? _____

4. Was it an EVEN chance?   Yes or No

Lesson 12: Honey Visits Grandpa Smith – Writing and Science

Content Area: Writing/Science

Grade Level: 1st - 2nd

Learning Standards: select and use writing processes for self-initiated and assigned writing;

develop abilities necessary to do a scientific inquiry in the field;

uses age-appropriate tools and models to verify that organisms and objects and parts of organisms and objects can be observed, described and measured.

Concepts: measurement, length, comparisons of lengths, comparative language, problem solving, answering questions

Time Frame: 50 minutes

MATERIALS AND RESOURCES:

1. *Honey's Visits Grandpa Smith* by Tom Greer
2. Attached handouts (3): one set per student
3. Writing and drawing utensils (pencils, pens, markers, crayons)
4. Large chart paper for teacher to write class story on
5. Magnifying glasses for students (1 per student or they can share on the exploration)
6. Ziploc or paper bags one per student
7. Area around school to walk and explore
8. Computers for students final drafts (if they choose)

OBJECTIVES:

The students will be able to...
1. Generate ideas for writing by using prewriting techniques, such as drawing and listing key thoughts
2. Develop a draft
3. Edit for appropriate grammar, spelling, punctuation and features of polished writings
4. Use a simple age-appropriate tool to observe and gather information
5. Demonstrate safe practices during field investigations

PRESENTATION/INTRODUCTION: attention getter

Ask the students, "Who likes to go on adventures?" "What kind of adventures do you like to go on?" "When you go on that adventure do you need to take anything special with you?" "What do you get to see, hear or touch on your adventure?" If, the students do not offer their own adventure stories, the teacher may share one of his/her own. Teacher can mention how adventures are fun, exciting, bring new experiences to you and sometimes you get to go back on the same adventures again. Teacher points to Honey and shows the cover of the book. "Honey will be going on her own adventure in this story. Let's see what happens. I wonder what she will need, see, hear and touch."

Show the cover of the book and read the title, author and illustrator. Show the back of the book, spine of the book and its title page. Compare the cover and title page: are they the same or different? Again, read the title of the book, the author and the illustrator to the students.

Teacher reads "Honey Visits Grandpa Smith" by Tom Greer. During the read aloud, the teacher should as questions or say things such as "I wonder what Honey needed to get to Grandpa Smith's house." "That sure is a whole lot of things for Honey to see and touch." When the teacher gets to the part of the story when Tommy and Grandpa Smith are talking, the teacher can mention how Honey could hear the.

Upon completion of the read aloud, the teacher will use the large chart paper to answer these questions:

1. What did Honey need to get to her adventure at Grandpas Smith's?
   Possible Answers: Tommy, car, gas

2. What did Honey see?
   Possible Answers: storage sheds, boxes, plates, bowls, stuffed animals

3. What did Honey hear?
   Possible Answers: the car, Tommy talking, Grandpa Smith talking, wind blowing

4. What did Honey touch?
   Possible Answers: the car, the grass, boxes, the ugly green floor, teddy bear, stuffed dog, etc.

Use the book as a reference for the students: as the student responds and verbally answers, turn to the page in the book or allow the student to find the pages. Once the list is complete, mention how all the things we listed were used to write the story and draw the pictures of this book (show book and flip through pages, point to pictures and words).

INTEREST BUILDING: why it is important

Ask students if they would like to go on an adventure? Tell them we will go on a Nature Adventure through our school. Mention we will need a few things before we go: magnifying glasses, a Ziploc/paper bag, and our rules. Demonstrate how to use a magnifying glass correctly and then hand one to each student. At this time, explain rules and expectations. Remind them we will be answering these questions when we return: what did we need, see, hear and touch.

Once outside, allow the students to explore grass, trees, plants, ant piles, any non-biting insects, birds, the sky, etc. Remind the students to use their magnifying glasses to get a closer view of different things. They may also pick up non-living items to place in their bags (i.e. sticks, leaves). Have students converse about what they are looking at, hearing, and touching. The teacher can help conversations along and delve deeper into student inquiry by offering assistive questions on whatever students are exploring.

CONTENT DEVELOPMENT: modeling/guided practice

1. Come back into the classroom and sit in a large circle with Ziploc/paper bags in front of the students.
2. Tell the students that they will now help answer these questions for the nature adventure: Write their answers on large chart paper.

What did we need to be able to go on our nature adventure here at school?

What did we see?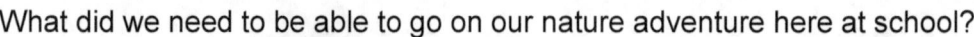

What did we hear?

What did we touch?

3. Now that the list is complete, we will begin to write a nature adventure story as a class but then the students will finish and illustrate it on their own. They will need to use items from their list to use in their story.
4. Begin the story with "We went on a nature walk around our school, today. We took our magnifying glasses with us to look at different things outside. We also got to take a bag to save some of our discoveries. (continue on…)
5. Now write these paragraph beginnings…
   ¶We saw…
   ¶We heard…
   ¶We touched…
   ….to help students with their drafts. A small discussion/brainstorming of what they may add in their story may occur at this point.
6. Remind them of the list we made earlier for Honey's adventure and the one we created for our adventure.
7. Students are to return to their seats, fill out their list sheet, write a short story, edit it and draw a picture about it.
8. If time permits, students may type up their stories.

SUMMARY/CLOSURE: review

1. Have volunteer students share their lists, stories and pictures in small groups.
2. Allow others to comment on the stories.
3. Review the lists to see what the students listed the same and what some of them listed that no-one else did.

EVALUATION: assess

1. Come back as a whole group and have students share either their lists, story or picture with everyone.
2. Ask the students why making these lists was important?
3. Did making the list help with your writing? How?
4. Did you like drawing the picture? Why or why not?

5. Why did we use magnifying glasses? What did it help you with?
6. Share what they learned from this writing experience.
7. What are some other adventures where it would be important to know what we would need before we went?
8. Continue the conversation with a new adventure i.e. an adventure to the beach. As a class, very shortly go through the listing process again. Point out, it is important to know what you may need before you go on an adventure. What if you went to the beach in a coat and blue jeans?

EXTENSION: center and homework

- Place a copy of each student's nature adventure story in the computer center to be typed out.
- Put all the stories and illustrations together in a class book and place it in the classroom library to be read and shared by everyone.
- Lay other adventure beginning stories in the language arts center so students may list, write and illustrate other adventures they have been on or would like to go on.

- Homework:

Draw a picture about a family adventure and write a short story.

"Honey Visits Grandpa Smith" 2nd grade Writing Lesson

On the nature adventure, I needed...

1.

2.

3.

On the nature adventure, I heard...

1.

2.

3.

On the nature adventure, I saw...

1.

2.

3.

On the nature adventure, I touched...

1.

2.

3.

"Honey Visits Grandpa Smith" 2nd grade Writing/Science Lesson

This is a picture of me on my nature adventure.

"Honey Visits Grandpa Smith" 2nd grade Writing/Science

This is a story about my nature adventure…

ABOUT THE AUTHOR

Dawn Lozano has been a teacher in the Corpus Christi, TX ISD since 2001. She taught at elementary level for eight years and is currently teaching Middle School Language Arts. She obtained her Bachelor of Science in 2001 and Master of Science in Curriculum and Instruction in 2007 at Texas A&M University – Corpus Christi. She currently resides in Corpus Christi with her pet Blue Heeler dog named Lily Pad Lozano.